T0001653

journey of a lifetime

Journey of a Lifetime

Discovering the Unique Adventure
God Has for You

taylor bennett

wander™
An imprint of
Tyndale House
Publishers

Visit Tyndale online at tyndale.com.

Visit the author online at taylor--bennett.com.

Tyndale and Tyndale's quill logo are registered trademarks of Tyndale House Ministries. *Wander* and the Wander logo are trademarks of Tyndale House Ministries. Wander is an imprint of Tyndale House Publishers, Carol Stream, Illinois.

Journey of a Lifetime: Discovering the Unique Adventure God Has for You

Designed by Lindsey Bergsma

Interior balloon images are the property of their respective copyright holders on Unsplash.com. Chapter 1 by Ian Dooley; Chapter 2 by Alex Azabache; Chapter 3 by Cinthia Aguilar; Chapter 4 by Benjamin Cremer; Chapter 5 by Maurits Bausenhart; Chapter 6 by Maximilian Meyer; Chapter 7 by Sven Scheuermeier; Chapter 8 by Cristina Gottardi; Chapter 9 by Max Harlynking.

For manufacturing information regarding this product, please call 1-855-277-9400.

For information about special discounts for bulk purchases, please contact Tyndale House Publishers at csresponse@tyndale.com, or call 1-855-277-9400.

Library of Congress Cataloging-in-Publication Data

A catalog record for this book is available from the Library of Congress.

ISBN 978-1-4964-5618-2

Printed in the United States of America

28	27	26	25	24	23	22
7	6	5	4	3	2	1

Jesus—this one's all for you

contents

ready for an adventure?

CIAO, FELLOW WANDERERS! If you're like me, you love the thrill of setting off on a new adventure, whether it's a flight around the world or just a stroll around the block. But did you know that the greatest journey you'll ever embark on doesn't happen via plane, train, car, bus, or boat?

In fact, the most important adventure of all time doesn't even take place outside your house. It happens within your heart.

It's your walk with God.

I knew from an early age that the Lord had given me *big* dreams and plans, but it was only when I learned to trust in him and devote my life to walking down his path that I began to fully understand those dreams and realize my passions. (In fact, those God-given dreams are what led me to write these words right now!)

If you've ever felt like God has something big planned for your life but you don't know what, or if you're having trouble knowing what path the Lord wants you to take, this book is for you. I started working on *Journey of a Lifetime* when I was dealing with a lot of uncertainty and change. As I wrote it, I began to immerse myself more fully in the Word until the Lord's plans for my life became clearer than I ever could have expected.

It is my hope and prayer that, as you journey alongside Jesus in the upcoming weeks, you will also experience God's guidance and provision on a whole new level. But, as with any truly great adventure, you can't begin your journey without first setting an itinerary. So let's talk a little bit about how this book works.

Journey of a Lifetime is divided into nine chapters, each of which focuses on a particular aspect of our journey with Christ and relates to a specific passage of Scripture. You'll find ten days' worth of devotions in each chapter, plus a special "bonus adventure" at the end. You can make this a true ninety-day experience, reading one devotion each day, *or* stretch it out by doing one devotion per day Monday through Friday and setting aside a day specifically for your bonus adventure at the end of every two-week period. Or if you're feeling particularly lost and could use some extra support, feel free to double up and read *two* devotions every day.

No matter what, every chapter comes packed with plenty of encouragement for your journey as well as a key verse to tuck in your bag for later. The first devotional of each chapter will introduce you to a small portion of Scripture I've selected just for you. Write it on a piece of paper with your nicest hand-lettering, scribble it on a note card, or scrawl it on the back of a receipt—whatever it takes!—then commit to memorizing it over the following weeks. By the end of this book, you'll be well equipped with several scriptural "souvenirs" that you can carry on your travels through this life—and cling to during difficult times.

This book is yours to do with as you please. It's simply a guidebook to help encourage you in your walk with the Lord. There's no right or wrong way to engage with it, and there's no pressure to follow a special formula. Our journey with Christ is never-ending yet ever changing, and so is this book. Keep it by your side as a companion during your journey, but keep the Lord and his Word even closer. Study the Scripture passages for yourself and learn from the words God gave to his people. It is my hope and prayer that this devotional will not only inspire you in your faith but also *challenge* you.

After all, setting off on an adventure can be a little daunting and arduous, but there is joy and beauty to be found in every step of every journey—especially our journey with the Lord!

As you work through this book and grow closer to God, I'd love to share in your journey via social media. Share your commitment to deepening your walk with the Lord with the hashtag #TakingTheJourneyOfALifetime, or tag me so I can come alongside you as you set off on this adventure.

Bon voyage!

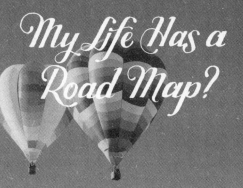

CHAPTER 1

My Life Has a Road Map?

DAY 1: JOURNEY OF A LIFETIME

READ JEREMIAH 1:4-10

> *Before I formed you in the womb I knew you,*
> *before you were born I set you apart. ~ v. 5*

SO YOU'RE READY to go on an adventure. I'm glad, because this isn't just any adventure. In fact, you've just taken the first step on a journey of a lifetime! Over the next ninety days, we're going to experience the crazy, powerful love of God firsthand and take a close look at the incredible, unique, and *amazing* plans he has for each and every one of us.

But before we can get started, we need a road map.

Any adventure—whether it's a cross-country trip or the great journey we call life—is only as good as the map we have to guide us. But finding a map of our city, state, or country is one thing. There isn't *really* a road map for our entire life.

Or is there?

The answer, my friends, is yes.

God knows each of us. Better than we know ourselves. And he loves us. Deeply. Powerfully. Eternally. Before we even entered this world, he put together a road map to guide us through this life: his Word. Along with that, the Lord has a map for each of our lives—a calling for us to live out that is far greater than we could ever imagine.

In this chapter, we'll be taking a closer look at these beautiful maps God has given us—both the one we find in the Bible and the one he's hidden away deep in our hearts. We'll explore verses that talk about his desire for us to follow his paths in obedience and trust, as well as those that highlight God's wild, unrivaled love for us.

Dear heavenly Father, what a joy and honor it is to know that you've given each of us a road map for our life. Thank you for being my Comforter and Protector, my Guide and my Friend. Give me the strength to follow the path you have laid out for me, and be with me in my heart and spirit today and every day. Amen.

To start things off, go ahead and write down today's memory verse—Jeremiah 1:5—and place it somewhere you'll see it often. Keep it close by your side as we embark on this incredible journey with the Creator of the world.

DAY 2: A LIGHT FOR OUR PATH

READ PSALM 119:101-105

Your word is a lamp for my feet,
a light on my path. ~ v. 105

PICTURE THIS: you're walking down a long country road under a sunset sky of blazing tangerine-orange and bubble gum–pink clouds. The air is cool with the promise of twilight, and birds sing their evening songs as they soar above the meadow. Peaceful, right?

Fast-forward a bit.

The sun has set, and darkness is creeping in. The birds have gone silent; the chill in the air is a bit more pronounced. Those cotton-candy clouds have gone as black as licorice, blotting out the moon and stars. A coyote howls in the distance. You're all alone.

When we try to go through life without God's Word, it can feel a bit like walking down that dark, deserted country road. Things become shadowy and scary without the light that comes from knowing him and being intimately acquainted with his promises.

In Psalm 119, the author tells us that God's Word is sweet like honey and that it illuminates the path he wants us to take.

If you feel like you've been walking in the dark lately, turn to the Lord and dig into the Bible. Not only will you find God's encouragement and truth on every page, but you'll also be gathering the wisdom you need to live out a life of faithfulness and obedience to him.

That alone makes this dark world just a little bit brighter.

Dear God, thank you for the guidance you've given us in the Bible. Give me a hunger for your Word today, Lord, and speak to me through it. Amen.

· ·

How can you make an effort to spend more time in God's Word? Write down some ideas here, then commit to trying one out for a week.

DAY 3: FOLLOW THE MAP

READ PROVERBS 3:1-8

> *He will make your paths straight.* ~ v. 6

I LOVE HIKING. Well, most of the time I love it.

But once, I set off on a hike that would supposedly take me to nearly a dozen gorgeous waterfalls via a simple seven-mile loop. Well, let me tell you, those seven miles turned into ten, and by the time I escaped from the maze that the "simple loop" had become, I was hungry, tired, and frustrated.

The hike sounded so easy. How could I possibly have gotten lost?

Simple: I'd forgotten to take a map. And, as I learned that day, even the most experienced hikers need something to guide them home.

The same is true in our lives. Even when we think we have everything figured out, there are still roadblocks, detours, and forks in the road. If we don't have a map, we're going to get—you guessed it—lost.

Thank goodness for our Savior, whose thoughts for us are more numerous than the stars in the sky and who already has a plan in place for each of us. When we align our own desires with what he has planned for our life and what he has ordained in his Word, we'll experience his peace and provision along the way.

But, at the same time, God understands that we're

human—aka *stubborn*. That's why he gives us a choice whether or not to accept all that he has in store for us. There have been times in my life when I've disobeyed what I knew was God's plan, and they all ended up about as well as my hiking experience.

That's not to say that God has us locked into an itinerary that takes us from day one all the way to heaven—we are free in Christ, and he gives us the freedom to make our own choices too. However, it's important for us to take all of our decisions before the Lord, prayerfully considering them and making sure they line up with the road map of his Word.

Today, let's make an effort to equip ourselves for the journey God is sending us on. When we obediently follow our Guide, we'll find that our journey is more beautiful than ever before.

Dear God, thank you for giving me the tools I need to find my way in this world through your Word and your perfect will. Forgive me for the times I've gone off track, and show me the way today. Amen.

....

Can you remember a time when your life went off track? How did you feel when you finally realigned yourself with God's guidance?

_____

_____

_____

_____

_____

_____

DAY 4: A CARNIVAL OF CHOICES

READ PSALM 143:7-12

> _Teach me the way in which I should walk;_
> _for to You I lift up my soul._ ~ v. 8 (NASB)

---○-○-○---

IF YOU'VE EVER visited a theme park or carnival, you probably know what it feels like to be overwhelmed. You enter through the main gate and are immediately met with sights and sounds and smells that all threaten to pull you in different directions. Should you take a picture with the guy in the giant animal costume, hop on a ride that will have you screaming like you're a little girl again, or head straight for the food cart with the amazing aromas?

Sometimes life can feel like that. We're tugged in all directions, each of them seemingly better and more intriguing than the next. When we're faced with some of life's BIG opportunities, it's easy to want to say yes to all of them. But, just as saying yes to everything at a carnival will leave you feeling exhausted, bloated, and even a bit motion sick (not to mention flat-out broke!), saying yes to every opportunity we come across can leave us feeling burned-out.

What if we remembered to turn to our Lord Jesus Christ when faced with an opportunity? What if we did as the psalmist said and listened for his faithfulness every day at the break of dawn? What then?

The more we seek God, the more he draws near to us. And as he draws near to us, he also begins to shape our paths and guide our lives. When we begin to intentionally seek his will and his plan, we are taking the first step in discovering his road map for our lives—the one that will lead to a bright, brilliant future.

The best part? Jesus is way cooler than any theme park character.

Dear Jesus, life is crazy for me today. I feel like I'm being pulled in a million directions, and I'm not sure where I should go. Please guide me and help me to do your will. Amen.

....

Every time you're faced with a decision today, take it to Jesus first. Pray for wisdom and guidance before giving an answer. At the end of the day, come back here and record what the experience was like.

_____

_____

_____

DAY 5: HAIRY SITUATIONS

READ JAMES 1:4-5

> *If any of you lacks wisdom, you should ask God,*
> *who gives generously to all without finding fault,*
> *and it will be given to you. ~ v. 5*

I DON'T KNOW about you, but I wouldn't consider myself especially wise. When I went on my first trip to Europe, I promptly blew up my only hair dryer, even after approximately 10,001 different sources had warned me not to plug it into a European outlet. I also assured my mom that the only way to get anywhere in Venice was to pay a water taxi almost a hundred dollars to take us half a mile down the canal, but that's a story for another time. (Sorry, Mom . . .) The point is, I don't always have a lot of that wonderful thing called wisdom.

But!

In God's Word, he reveals to us that he will *give* wisdom to all those who ask for it. What a relief! Of course, that doesn't mean we'll be exempt from making some really dumb decisions (like trying to plug in that hair dryer). We're still human, after all.

Besides, his wisdom doesn't usually come to us as a big red warning label on an electrical outlet. It isn't written in the sky, waiting for us to look up and take heed. Instead, God's wisdom comes as a gentle prodding, a whisper in our spirit that nudges us in the right direction. It comes from spending time in his Word and learning to live in obedience to him. There is such freedom to be found in this still, small voice that lifts us up and helps us live for Christ.

That's because godly wisdom is meant to guide us—to ensure that we're living lives that are glory-filled and God-honoring. Godly wisdom isn't a command that we have to follow or a set of rules. Godly wisdom is a way of life.

When we live in obedience and faithfulness to the Lord, we will come to understand his Word in a way that equips us to make choices that will not only please our Father in heaven but also guide us further down the path he has for us. This sort of wisdom is such a gift, and it's ours for the taking—all we need to do is ask.

Dear God, I need your wisdom. Help me to see the world through your eyes. Guide my steps and direct my path, and give me the power to make choices that reflect your desires for my life. Amen.

What is one area of your life in which you could use a bit of heavenly wisdom? Write it down here, then commit to asking God for help several times a day. Listen for his still, small voice as you wait for an answer.

_____

_____

_____

_____

_____

_____

_____

_____

DAY 6: TSUNAMI WATCH

READ JAMES 1:6-8

You must believe and not doubt, because the one who doubts is like a wave of the sea, blown and tossed by the wind. - v. 6

CLOSE YOUR EYES and picture this. (Wait—don't *actually* close your eyes, because then you wouldn't be able to read. . . .)

You're sitting on a beach on a tropical island, digging your toes into the sand and tilting your face to meet the golden sunshine as ocean waves crash on the shore in front of you. All is peaceful; all is calm. Suddenly—out of nowhere—a gust of wind whips up, throwing the peaceful waves into a wild, rocky rhythm. Soon the water is inching up higher and higher on the sand. It's headed straight toward you.

Sneaker waves and riptides can rise at a moment's notice, and when the winds pick up, it's a sure bet that the ocean is growing more tumultuous by the minute. So, too, if we don't surrender our fears and trust in God, we will be buffeted on every side by the wicked winds of this world.

Yesterday we read about God's incredible gift of wisdom in the book of James—but the same chapter goes on to say we must not doubt that God will provide that gift; when we ask for wisdom, we must *believe* that it will come.

Just like we wouldn't buy a road map only to decide that it can't be trusted, we can't ask God for his gift of wisdom only to turn around and start doubting it. God is our loving heavenly Father, the author and perfecter of our faith. His plans for us are for good and not for evil—so we can trust that his plan for our life is far greater than we could ever imagine.

And what a relief that is! Honestly, it's easy to feel overwhelmed by the mere *thought* of attempting to discern God's will for our lives. There are so many possibilities to consider, opportunities that arise, and decisions to make. It's easy to lose faith that we truly are walking down the right path. And that's where the Lord comes in. Because, no matter what, when we serve and honor him, our journey is sure to be one of beauty and grace.

With God's wisdom reigning in our hearts, we have nothing to fear. Our Father loves us, and he is ready to give us good gifts when we live a life of faithfulness to him.

Dear Jesus, I love you. Help me put my trust in you more and more each day so I might receive the incredible gifts you have in store for me. Help me grow in wisdom, strength, and courage as I walk down the path you have planned for me.

....

What can you do today to exercise your trust in the Lord?

_____

_____

_____

_____

_____

_____

_____

DAY 7: TRAVEL PLANS

READ PSALM 33

> *But the plans of the LORD stand firm forever,*
> *the purposes of his heart through all generations.* ~ v. 11

I LOVE MAKING PLANS—especially when I go on a trip. Since I was young, I've been the family concierge, doing research, drawing out multiple itineraries, and making restaurant reservations weeks (sometimes even months!) in advance. But, without fail, when we finally reach our destination, those plans go out the window one way or another. There's just no way to fully anticipate actually *being* in a certain location. The lure of street food, the call to explore the unknown, and the everyday mishaps that come with an adventure never fail to send us in a completely different direction from the one listed on my carefully drawn-out itinerary.

Thank goodness that our God is nothing like me! As it says in the Psalms, his heart's desire for us was written long before we were even born. His plans for our lives are unchangeable—unshakable. The Lord doesn't change his mind; we can trust that his Word and the plans he has for us will not waver. They are good, and they're everlasting.

The next time we feel uncertainty creeping in about our season in life, let's turn to the Lord. We can ask him what he has for us in this time. And—best of all—we can take heart that, whatever his answer is, it is good. It is *true*. His map for us was drawn before time began, and we can trust in him for all eternity.

Lord God, what a beautiful gift you have given me! Thank you for giving me a plan for my life that never changes and never fails. Please show me what you have for me, and help me to walk down your path.

....

Take some time this week to go on a trip down memory lane—pull out an old photo album or two and look back over pictures of your childhood. Think about your dreams and plans back then, and compare those dreams with your current hopes and goals. How has God used certain events in your life to keep you walking down the path he's set out for you?

_____

_____

_____

_____

_____

_____

DAY 8: NEVER ALONE

READ PSALM 139

> *If I rise on the wings of the dawn, if I settle on the far side of the sea, even there your hand will guide me. ~ vv. 9-10*

○○○

WHERE DO YOU want to live when you grow up? Are you a hometown girl, or do you yearn for the adventure of moving to a new city, state, or even country? I've always dreamed of moving to Italy and teaching English—or becoming a full-time travel blogger and sharing my globe-trotting experiences with the world—but, for now, God is keeping me busy right in my little hometown in the PNW (Pacific Northwest). And, much as I love the *idea* of living somewhere new and exotic, this homebody is happy to stay put.

What a comfort it is to know that wherever we are—whether that's our bedroom or a jet airplane thousands of miles above the Pacific Ocean—God is right there with us. Similarly, no matter if we feel like we're on top of the world or in the deepest valley, he is there, guiding us and whispering his plans into our hearts. No matter where we go, we cannot escape his presence.

That might seem like an intimidating thought at first, but it is also wonderful.

The God who made heaven and earth is standing by our side—neither leaving nor forsaking us—and walking along with us through every step of this crazy journey called life. He loves us, cares for us, and has gifted us with his Word, the best road map a girl could ask for.

Jesus, thank you for your presence, for being with me no matter the circumstances. This journey of life has many twists and turns, yet you remain faithful through everything. Guide me today, I pray. Amen.

....

If you could travel anywhere in the world, where would you go? How do you think God could use you to bless others in that place? Below, dream a little about the limitless possibilities , then write about one place you're going today. How can you listen to God's prompting and follow him when you're there?

_____

_____

_____

_____

_____

_____

DAY 9: GPS GLITCH

READ EPHESIANS 1:15-23

> *I pray that the eyes of your heart may be enlightened in order that you may know the hope to which he has called you, the riches of his glorious inheritance in his holy people.* – v. 18

HAVE YOU EVER tried to follow a GPS while driving down a crowded city street or strolling along a bustling sidewalk? You might be attempting to follow the directions, but your eyes are constantly drawn to the hubbub around you. I'll never forget when my mom and I tried to find our way back to our hotel during our first night in Venice. Every cobbled alleyway looked alike, and try as we might to pay attention to the map on my phone, we couldn't keep from getting distracted by the unusual sights, sounds, and smells of the city.

Like the magical floating city of Venice, this life is filled with myriad things that can distract us from our goal. Even when we're doing our best to keep our eyes on God and his plans for us, the world can so easily divert our attention elsewhere. The lure of sin—of perfectionism, dishonesty, gossip, or something else entirely—can cripple us in our walk with the Lord.

That's why Paul prayed that the hearts of his fellow believers would be enlightened—so that they could fully understand the great gift of salvation. When we remember what's at the end of this life's journey—eternal life with Christ!—our focus is dramatically changed.

Life with Christ will be greater than any five-star resort, more beautiful than any secluded campground. Eternal life itself is our final destination. It is *real*.

If you're struggling to stay on course with God's plan for your life today, remember that this world is not our final destination. This life is only the journey. The independence God has given us here to explore the world and discover his plan for us is nothing compared to the freedom we will find in the new creation, once Jesus returns to make everything right again. We will no longer be tempted to sin by the devil. Everything will be bright and fresh—clean and new. *Someday.*

God, open my eyes. Help me to see this life for what it is—a long, imperfect journey to the perfect world you have planned for us. Let me honor you with my thoughts and actions and keep my eyes fixed on you. Guide me today, God. I love you.

When do you feel pulled away from closely following God? What is one small change you can make in your life that will help you stay on track?

_____

_____

_____

_____

_____

_____

DAY 10: THE ULTIMATE GUIDEBOOK

READ HEBREWS 4:12-13

> *For the word of God is alive and active. – v. 12*

WHEN I WAS TWELVE YEARS OLD, my aunt got me a Maui guidebook for Christmas. She knew that I would soon be visiting the island for the very first time with my family and that I was eagerly planning my trip. Over the next few months, as I prepared to fly halfway across the Pacific Ocean (my first big flight!), that guidebook was my constant companion. I read it over and over again, dog-earing pages and taking notes on must-see locations and attractions. In the years since that magical Maui trip, I have continued to use travel guidebooks and blogs to help me plan every one of my trips—even when I'm going on a day trip.

What if we treated our Bibles more like I treated that old guidebook? What if we got our own copy, read it through—multiple times—and took every part of it to heart? If you're like me, you might've shied away from Bible reading before because it seems boring (reading through old family trees isn't exactly at the top of my must-do list). But what if we saw God's Word for exactly what it is—real, relevant, and powerful, even today? What would happen if we were to cling to the Bible with the same urgency with which we rely on a map or GPS during a road trip?

God has a special plan for each one of us; he is ready and waiting to guide us. When we live according to his Word, we can rest in the confidence that we are walking down the right path.

God, thank you for the gift of your Word. Help me to lean on it and use it as a guide as I navigate through my life. When what I read doesn't seem to make sense or have a purpose, open my heart and give me the wisdom to understand your Word. Amen.

....

Make your Bible—your spiritual guidebook—*yours*. Mark it up, dog-ear the pages, or take notes in a separate journal. Don't just read the Word; immerse yourself in it!

bonus adventure: start mapping!

We've spent a lot of time talking about the road map of God's Word and the way it helps us follow him and discover his route for our lives. The Lord knows our next step even before we do, and the more we delight ourselves in him and spend time in his presence, the more we'll come to see those plans at work in our lives. Today, why don't you set aside some time to do just that?

Whether you've already started to see God's plan for you reveal itself or you still feel completely map-less, let these questions be a jumping-off point for you as you prayerfully consider the amazing things God has planned for your life.

- Where has God placed me right now?

- What might he want from me in this situation?

- Where do I want to go?

- Does this seem like somewhere God might want me?

- What are my passions?

- How might God use those passions to impact the world for good?

- What does my relationship with God look like right now? Do I feel like I'm following his will or forging my own trail?

- How can I spend more time studying the map that he has given me through his Word?

CHAPTER 2

Which Gate?

DAY 1: TWO ROADS

READ MATTHEW 7:13-20

> *Small is the gate and narrow the road that leads to life,*
> *and only a few find it. - v. 14*

IF YOU'VE EVER visited a massive airport, like LAX in Los Angeles or LHR in London, you've experienced firsthand the frenzy of trying to find your gate. LAX has well over one hundred gates spread out across eight different terminals. I'll never forget the near-panicked feeling of trying to make it from one LAX terminal to the next on a shuttle bus to catch a connecting flight . . . *after* I'd spent the last fourteen hours on a flight from London *and* gone through customs. Yikes!

Making it to my next gate was nothing short of stressful that day, but the task of finding the "narrow gate" that Jesus talks about in today's reading can be just as intimidating.

I don't know about you, but when I think about the path to eternal life, more often than not, I end up picturing a semi-magical Jacob's ladder, surrounded by rainbows and sparkly, silver-lined clouds. But in all reality, the road to eternal life is never described as attractive or easy. In fact, in this passage, the route to heaven is described as small, narrow, and hard to find. Not exactly full of sparkles and rainbows, is it?

Add to that the fact that there's another path—one that's wide and welcoming—and it's easy to get off track on our journey with the Lord.

But what does this path to destruction look like? Why is it so enticing? And most importantly, how can we avoid it?

We're going to be taking a closer look at all of those questions and more in the days ahead, but let's take care of one thing first:

Sin leads to death.

That, in a nutshell, is what Jesus is talking about in this passage. If we live lives built on a foundation of sin—of sneakiness and selfishness and a bunch of other *baaaad* things—we're building our own tomb even as we live. Yes, we all go astray, but when we willingly choose to spend our lives riding down the open road of sin, we're going to reach a destination that is anything but appealing.

However, if we stay away from sin and its enticements that

society has branded as "cool" (gossip, laziness, etc.), we'll find something so much better at the end of our road. Living a life that glorifies our Savior might not be easy. It can feel downright hard at times, especially when peer pressure kicks in. But it leads to glorious rewards, not only in heaven but also on this earth.

Let's start walking down the narrow path!

Dear Lord, thank you for giving me road signs through your Word to help me find and stay on the narrow path. Help me to not stray onto the path of sin but, instead, keep me walking according to your ways. Amen.

....

Write this chapter's key verse on an index card and make a point to read over it throughout your day. Use the card as a reminder that what seems right in the moment isn't always what glorifies our Savior. Take the Lord's words to heart, and remind yourself of them whenever you're faced with a proverbial fork in the road.

DAY 2: PLEASING PEOPLE OR PLEASING GOD?

READ GALATIANS 1:6-10

> *Am I now trying to win the approval of*
> *human beings, or of God? ~ v. 10*

DID YOU ENJOY playing dress-up when you were little? I know I did. In fact, I still do! So, naturally, when I went to Europe for the first time, I went to great pains (literally) to avoid committing a fashion faux pas while in France. A bit of pre-trip research had me 100 percent convinced that I would be branded a "tacky tourist" if I dared to wear even the nicest pair of flip-flops.

And so, when my mom and I stepped off the cruise ship and onto the cobbled streets of Marseille, she was wearing comfy flip-flops, and I was wearing ankle booties. Not comfortable walking or hiking boots, mind you, but booties. With heels. By the time I got back to the cruise ship (having walked upwards of fourteen miles!) after one of my French excursions, I wondered if my feet would ever walk again.

Okay, so I'm being overdramatic, but you get the picture. I'd let the French conventions and a bit of silly pride keep me from doing what I knew I should've done—worn shoes that *wouldn't* have killed my feet. Unfortunately, somewhere along the way, I let my desire to fit in and not stick out like a tacky tourist override common sense.

We do that a lot, don't we? Give in to peer pressure even when God has instructed us to stand strong in what we believe? It's something that we as Christians know better than to do, but it's a lot easier said than done.

Not even the ancient church was immune to this kind of pressure. When false teachers offered advice that didn't align with Scripture, many members of the church at Galatia began "quickly deserting" the gospel that had been preached to them. You and I might not experience the same kinds of temptations and pressures as these long-ago believers, but we still face peer pressure on an all-too-regular basis.

It's often easy for us to give in to persuasion—not just pressure from our friends but promises from the media. We're sure to become so much cooler if only we do this, buy that, or get involved in whatever's trending at the moment. And, while doing any or all of these things may give us a temporary boost in popularity, that's not really what we should be focusing on in the first place. Instead, we should be striving, as Paul did, to win the approval of God—not other people.

The Lord's favor is far superior to compliments from the world, and entering into his Kingdom is infinitely better than being well-liked. What's waiting for us on the other side of this life is so much sweeter than even a drop of momentary popularity. Even now, knowing Jesus is the ultimate gift, one that is a thousand times more satisfying than finding acceptance from the world. As we journey through this chapter, let's focus less on our earthly image and more on how we can ready ourselves for his Kingdom.

Dear God, it's so easy for me to get caught up in trying to win the approval of others. Please help me to seek to honor you first and foremost. Give me strength to resist negative peer pressure, I pray. Amen.

....

The next time you feel pressured to do something that makes you uncomfortable, take it before the Lord and ask yourself, *Would doing this gain me approval in the eyes of my friends or in God's eyes?* Start putting him first in your decision-making, and watch it revolutionize your life!

DAY 3: BE TRANSFORMED

READ ROMANS 12:1-2

> *Do not conform to the pattern of this world, but be transformed by the renewing of your mind. - v. 2*

THERE'S A SORT OF Hawaii tourism pattern that most people follow. It usually includes a trip to—you guessed it—a luau; a surfing lesson that could possibly leave a person seasick; and an inordinate amount of artificially flavored shave ice. This commercialized Hawaiian vacation itinerary that's heavily promoted by every piece of tourist literature in every airport kiosk might sound well and good—and it can be fun—but it's not the most authentic experience you can have.

In order to really encounter and appreciate the true Hawaii, you have to be willing to toss out those glossy brochures and dive deeper into the wonders that the islands have to offer. When I travel to Hawaii, I usually find that it's far more exciting to forgo the usual flashy (and oftentimes expensive!) tourist attractions in favor of a quiet walk on the beach. While strolling the beach, I have the opportunity to collect tiny shells—the ultimate souvenirs—and feel the sand scrape between my toes. The *right* beach (usually a local park rather than a resort beachfront) even offers me a taste of local life. There might be stray chickens wandering about, families picnicking, or even a school's outrigger canoe club practicing right offshore.

I always have a remarkably more meaningful vacation when I steer clear of tourist traps and engage in more authentic activities. But did you know that we, as Christians, are called to avoid the world's tourist traps too?

When we conform to society's expectations, fighting to impress our peers or doing stuff just because it's the cool thing to do, we aren't living to honor the Lord—we're living to impress others. Instead of going with the flow and living the way "everybody else" does, why don't we search the Scriptures to discover how *God* wants us to live?

Day in and day out, we're bombarded by messages not all that different from the ones we see on travel brochures. They promise us that by doing X, Y, or Z; buying a specific product; or acting a certain way, we will somehow magically earn the world's approval. But approval from the world is cheap—easy to come by and even easier to lose.

Instead, let's challenge ourselves to seek *God's* approval by doing what he asks of us. Rather than chasing after the temporal, let's do as Paul urges us in Romans. Let's stop conforming and be *transformed*.

Dear God, it's easy for me to get caught up in trying to fit in with what the world promises is good. Help me to fix my mind on you and your Kingdom. Let me know and understand and do more of your will, I pray. Amen.

....

The next time you feel torn about a decision you have to make, take the issue before the Lord. Ask yourself, *What does God want me to do?* Often, the answer is clearer than we think!

DAY 4: GOOD COMPANY

READ 1 CORINTHIANS 15:30-34

> *Do not be misled:*
> *"Bad company corrupts good character." ~ v. 33*

DO ME A FAVOR and take a mental vacation with me—just for a minute. Close your eyes and imagine an ancient Greek version of the "bad side" of Las Vegas. You know what I mean. Now scatter around a bunch of temples devoted to various idols and an unhealthy obsession with lawsuits, and you've got a pretty good idea of what exactly the debauched ancient city of Corinth was like.

In other words?

Ancient Corinth wasn't the kind of place you'd want to take the family for a fun-filled vacation.

Imagine the struggle, then, of trying to live an upright and godly life in a place like that when you were constantly bombarded with disturbing images and temptations and popularized idol worship . . .

Wait a minute.

In reality, ancient Corinth wasn't much different from today's society. Oh, sure, our idols today (perfect grades, social media, popularity, etc.) might not be monumentalized in temples or carved out of stone, but they're idols nonetheless—ones that we deal with on a daily basis.

As Christians, we have an opportunity to rise above this fallen, broken world and live for God no matter what. But that can be hard to do when the people we're hanging out with have values that don't reflect what the Lord wants for us.

See, there's this thing called *acculturation*. If you spend enough time immersed in one culture or another, you'll naturally start to adopt certain aspects of that way of life. For example, when I went to Europe I came home a bread snob. After only two short weeks of eating fresh-baked artisan loaves, my tastes had changed forever.

Of course, acculturation isn't always a bad thing. It can actually be very good. If you've experienced the rush that comes from spending time with fellow believers at church camp or on a mission trip, you probably know what I'm talking about.

However, when we hang out with people who don't share our values—who might even try to pressure us into making decisions that we *know* aren't right—we're placing ourselves in great danger.

When we spend the majority of our time with people who aren't living the kind of life God has called us to, we're opening our hearts and minds to a whole host of unhealthy behaviors. Naturally, many of our friends, coworkers, and even family members will have different convictions than we do. And while it's important for us to spend time with them and share the light of Jesus, we also must stand firm in our own beliefs and cultivate Christian friendships to counteract the world's influences. When we spend time surrounded by "bad company," we must ensure that our own "good morals" stay centermost in our minds.

After all, acculturation is a two-way street. If we stand strong against what we know is wrong and live for the Lord in all situations, there's a chance that we just might begin winning over others' hearts for Jesus. The time that we take to spread God's good news to others might be just what they need to make the decision to follow him.

Dear Lord, it's hard to find friends whose character reflects what you want from me. Help me to build relationships that glorify and honor you, and help me to stand firm in my own convictions when I'm spending time with those who don't share my faith. Use me as a light for you no matter where I'm at. Amen.

Think about your friend group—would you classify the people in it as "good company" or "bad company"? Are your traveling companions helping or hindering your journey?

_____

_____

_____

DAY 5: ETERNAL PERSPECTIVE

READ MATTHEW 6:19-24

No one can serve two masters. ~ v. 24

FOR MY BIRTHDAY ONE YEAR, my mom gifted me a girls' trip in the form of a "relaxing getaway" to a small town a couple of hours away. She booked us a cozy cottage with a quiet, tranquil backyard, and we brought plenty of books to read and games to play as we soaked in the peace and quiet.

But when we got to the town, we realized that there was so much to do—massive public gardens to walk through, quaint downtown shops to peruse, quirky little cafés to dine at, and so much more! We ended up exploring all day, every day. By the time we headed home, I'd begun to feel like I needed a vacation *from* my vacation!

In this world we're often torn between two "masters," as the Bible calls them. Some of these tough decisions don't matter much in the grand scheme of things (the choice between spending a weekend tucked away in a cozy cottage or exploring an enchanting small town doesn't exactly have eternal consequences . . .), but other choices *do* matter. A lot.

In today's passage, Jesus is specifically talking about the danger of the love of money, but his words ring true in relation to a million different things. Anything that we let into our life—be it a job, a hobby, or even a relationship—has the potential to become a passion. And while it's certainly not bad to have passions, we need to be careful to keep them in check.

The second those things overshadow our one true passion (that's Jesus Christ) we're in danger of letting the Lord take second (or third or even fourth) place in our life. Honestly, sometimes it's way easier to pin our hearts and hopes and dreams on something that is right in front of us. Something we can touch. It can be hard to cling to our invisible tour guide when our attentions are captured by the thrill and urgency of the here and now.

It's during times like these that we have to step back and search for that eternal perspective—the one that acknowledges the journey we're on and will point us back to Jesus. Because even though we can't see or feel or hear the Lord the way we can other people, he is there. He's more real than our other passions or even our greatest fears.

When Jesus died on the cross, he paid the ultimate price for us. He captured our hearts with his love. When we choose to serve him above all else, we are not only giving him the glory and honor he deserves, but we are also aligning our priorities in a way that will fill our hearts and lives with the light that comes only from him.

As we walk along this road together, let's remember which path we're on—and glorify the one who is guiding us through it all.

Dear Lord, you know how hard it can be for me to keep my eyes on you when so many other things in life vie for my attention. Help me remember to put you above all else, and forgive me for the times when I don't. Amen.

....

What are your priorities for this coming week? How does the Lord fit into those? Have you set aside time for prayer, devotions, or Bible reading? If not, reevaluate your schedule to give God the high place of honor that he deserves.

_____

_____

_____

_____

_____

_____

_____

_____

DAY 6: WALK WITH HIM

READ MICAH 6:6-9

> *What does the LORD require of you but to do justly, to love mercy, and to walk humbly with your God? – v. 8 (NKJV)*

ONE OF MY FAVORITE THINGS to do whenever I go *anywhere* is to take a walk. I love stepping out of my hotel room, cottage, or condo (or even my own house!) and setting off on an exploratory adventure. Whether I amble down city side streets, stroll along secluded paths, or simply meander down an unfamiliar road in my own hometown, I always find a certain charm in exploring my surroundings on foot.

Maybe that's why I've always loved the passage in Genesis in which the Lord is described as "walking in the garden in the cool of the day" (3:8). I can just close my eyes and picture the Lord wandering through the Garden with his people. What wonders they must have seen, and what mysteries they must have talked about!

Because of the sin committed in the Garden that fateful day, we're no longer able to physically stroll side by side with God, but we are still called to walk with him. Today's passage in Micah gives us an intimate look at what the Lord desires most from us—our hearts.

God does not ask that we come before him with elaborate prayers or costly sacrifices or pretentious displays of knowledge. Instead, what the Lord requires is that we love others in a merciful, fair, and humble way. That we cling to pure and godly things, not to the "treasures of wickedness" that are mentioned later in Micah chapter 6.

As Christians, we are called to *walk with the Lord*. The Bible doesn't say "hang out with the in crowd" or "go with the flow." In fact, many times it states the contrary! Many of history's greatest Christians were despised and mocked by others here on earth, but they're now enjoying true glory in God's Kingdom.

Remember this chapter's key verse? There are two gates to choose between—two paths to walk. One is an easy road, filled with the pleasures of this world. It's easy to find and easy to stay on . . . but, friends, it doesn't lead to eternal life.

When we walk with the Lord, we're not guaranteed a smooth road. In fact, we're told that the path to eternal life is narrow. Sometimes we might lose our way. The markers of success, popularity, and acceptance might be few and far between—or missing altogether. But you know who's never missing?

Jesus Christ himself.

Dear God, sometimes it seems easier to walk in the ways of this world instead of following in your footsteps. Please help me to follow your lead more and more as I grow in my relationship with you.

....

Below are two different paths. Fill in one path with all the ways that you can honor God—respecting your parents, reading the Bible, etc.—and the other path with choices that could lead to destruction—disobeying your parents, talking behind someone's back, etc. Which path would you rather go down? Which path are you on right now?

Path 1

_____

_____

_____

_____

_____

Path 2

_____

_____

_____

_____

_____

_____

_____

_____

DAY 7: NOT THERE YET

READ JOHN 17:6-26

They are not of the world, even as I am not of it. ~ v. 16

I ALWAYS HAVE a bit of a hard time on the last day of a vacation—or even summer break! Waking up that morning and preparing to turn the page to a new chapter of life always gives me a strange sense of restlessness. I would give anything to be able to pause time—to spend just another day in my happy place, the one my heart has learned to call home—but I can't. At the same time, I haven't reached my new destination either. I feel, in a sense, lost.

Sometimes we can feel this way about regular life, too. After all, we read in today's featured passage that this world is not our home. When Jesus prayed for his disciples on the night before his crucifixion, he didn't think of them as ordinary men. He saw them as beloved and set apart. So, too, are we. When we accept Jesus' great gift of salvation, we are no longer of this world.

God has called us to eternal life with him. Yet, for the foreseeable future, we're living in a fallen world. But he says that we are not *of* this world. And all that can leave us feeling a little . . . caught in between.

How can we make ourselves at home in the waiting before Jesus returns and makes all things new? Sadly, many of us try so hard to make this earth our home that we lose focus on our citizenship in heaven. By trying to walk the wide, easy path and honor God at the same time, we're essentially attempting to live two separate lives.

It might feel as if we're in limbo, hovering between our heavenly home and the here and now, but really, we're not. We are called to eternal life in Christ, and if you know him as your Savior, that life has already begun!

Because of God's promise to us, we can stop living with

half of our heart here and the other half in heaven. Instead, we can devote our hearts completely to doing the Lord's work. The rest of the world might not understand this. We might be tempted to follow along with those who don't share our God-given beliefs, but there is so much more waiting for us when we choose to walk in God's perfect plan.

We have been given a heavenly inheritance—a future home with God and all of his people—and, until that day, we can do everything in our power to show the world what God's Kingdom is like. By staying on the path God has laid out for us and reflecting him to the people in our lives, we're not only staying the course. We're paving the way for more hearts to follow after God and his will.

Dear Lord, what a comfort it is to know that I wasn't called to fit in but to stand out. When it gets hard for me to stay on the narrow path, help me to see that I was called to something more—that this life is not my own and this world is not my home. I can't wait to spend eternity with you! Amen.

....

Have you ever felt out of place? How can the knowledge that your true citizenship is in heaven help explain the way you felt then?

_____

_____

_____

_____

_____

_____

DAY 8: TREASURE HUNTING

READ DEUTERONOMY 14:1-2

> *The LORD has chosen you to be his treasured possession.* ~ v. 2

WHAT'S YOUR FAVORITE THING to do at the beach? Are you the first one in the water, splashing in the waves and bodysurfing until sundown, or do you prefer to spread out your blanket and catch some rays? Maybe you'd rather help a younger sibling construct a massive sand castle or take a long walk along the shoreline, looking for treasures.

While I've been known to do all of the above during a single day at the beach, I'm particularly fond of beachcombing. There's something about collecting tiny snippets of God's handiwork—be they sea-frosted bits of glass, discarded hermit crab abodes, or water-tumbled agates—that never grows old. I've even been known to go treasure hunting for unusual stones along the banks of the river that runs through my hometown. And no matter whether I've been exploring a tropical beach or the local riverbank, I always manage to find a handful (er, bagful) of special treasures to call my very own.

When I read today's key verse in Deuteronomy, I can't help but picture God as a sort of benevolent beachcomber, choosing his people to be his treasure. Special. Set apart.

God sees us as precious, and he has great plans for each of us. That's why he has called us to go on this incredible journey of faith. And that's why we are walking the narrow path.

If you've trusted Jesus to save you—to deliver you from your sins—he did so for good. He welcomed you into his family and placed you on a new path. In the same way that I store the treasures I collect while beachcombing in a special dish or jar, God has prepared a special place for those who know and love him.

But today's passage in Deuteronomy isn't just a comforting reminder for God's people. It goes deeper than that. The writer of this passage didn't want the ancient Israelites (his original audience) simply to understand their incredible relationship with their heavenly Father. He wanted them to see that, as members of God's family, they had been called to live holy and upright lives.

Though we might never be tempted to shave the front of our heads in an expression of grief, this was a common practice among pagan nations. By forbidding this kind of action, the Lord was essentially speaking out against idol worship and setting the Israelites apart from the rest of the world.

God has called us out of sin and darkness to make us his very own. Why, then, would we want to engage in activities that lead us back into the fallen world from which we came? Instead, as Christ's children, let's become a reflection not of the world, but of him.

Let's remember our identity as God's treasures.

Dear God, knowing that I am loved and treasured by you is one of the greatest feelings in the world. Thank you for rescuing me from my sins. Help me to live a life that reflects your love and not the ways of this world. Amen.

....

What things do you do because "everybody else does them"? It might be watching a show with mature content, cheating on your homework, making fun of a classmate behind her back, or something else entirely. How do these choices cause you to pull away from your identity as one of God's treasured possessions?

_____

_____

_____

_____

_____

_____

_____

_____

_____

DAY 9: SINKING CITY

READ 1 JOHN 2:15-17

Whoever does the will of God lives forever. ~ *v. 17*

DID YOU KNOW that the city of Venice is sinking?

After eight hundred years of standing on "stilts" in the Venetian Lagoon, the ancient buildings that draw tens of millions of visitors each year are getting a little tired. Some of the most pessimistic experts estimate that it will be less than a hundred years before this beloved Italian city of music and gondolas and canals will be completely submerged!

Whether or not this will actually happen, it's a poignant reminder that nothing on this earth will last forever. In fact, it's quite the opposite. This world—and everything in it—is doomed to destruction through the sin of humankind. There will come a time when Jesus will return and put an end to the world as we know it. But we as Christians have been given such an incredible gift in our relationship with God—eternal life on the *new* earth to come.

In today's passage, the apostle John pleads with Christians to stand firm in the faith, not to let any passing distractions keep them from fulfilling their true purpose. While this was an important message for the on-fire ancient church, it's equally relevant for those of us who live in today's fast-paced, short-sighted society.

We are told in today's passage that worldly pleasures can

interfere with our ability to follow God wholeheartedly. We can't take anything out of this world—not possessions, not wealth, not fame. When Jesus Christ brings us home to be with him, we can just take one thing: ourselves.

Though we can leave a legacy on earth through our kind words and actions, the only things we can bring with us when we leave are those that already reside within our hearts.

What are we carrying along the road of life? Are we grasping tightly to temporal things—which will bring us joy in the present yet will all disappear in the blink of an eye? Or are we filling our hearts with the desires that God has given us? Desires to live for Christ. To help and serve others. To walk the narrow path.

This doesn't mean we're not supposed to enjoy life—to build God-honoring relationships and do great things here on this earth—but it *does* require us to keep those things from overtaking the real reason we're here. God placed us on this earth and called us into his Kingdom because he loves us. He wants us to focus on things of eternal importance, even in our everyday lives.

Let's leave behind our worldly cares today and focus on the path before us—the road that leads straight to the everlasting.

Dear God, it's so easy to get caught up in concerns that don't really matter in the long run. Help me to live more for you and less for the temptations and charms of this world. Forgive me for the times when I let my passions and possessions overtake my love for you, and help me to remember where my true home is. Amen.

What things matter most to you right now? Write them down below, then rate them in order of importance. Where does your heavenly Father rank on this list?

_____

_____

_____

_____

_____

_____

_____

_____

DAY 10: LIFT EACH OTHER UP

READ ECCLESIASTES 4:9-12

Two are better than one. . . . If they fall,
one will lift up his companion. ~ vv. 9-10 (NKJV)

I'M NOT EXACTLY Miss Graceful. One time when my mom and I were taking a walk in the sunshine, I tripped over a crack in the sidewalk and flew right into the air. I'd like to say that my moment of disgrace ended then, but it didn't. That only happened after I had splatted fantastically—almost face-first—onto the same sidewalk from which I had flown.

I crashed down hard, earning myself several cuts and bruises and one *very* sore elbow. In that moment, I was beyond thankful that my mom was there with me. She helped me to my feet and dusted me off and was generally a great comfort in the middle of a lot of pain.

If I could biff it that bad on a sunlit pathway, then we're all guaranteed to stumble as we walk down this road of life. And not just once, but many, many times. (Why do you think the apostle Paul referred to the Christian journey as a race to be run with perseverance?)

Not only is the path to eternal life narrow and hard to find, but it's also filled with stumbling blocks placed there by the enemy. We're going to get lost. We're going to get tripped up. We're going to fall. That's why I *love* today's passage from Ecclesiastes. It is such a clear picture of the kind of relationships we need to have on this earth in order to complete our journey of faith.

We've talked a lot in this chapter about the kind of people we travel with. We're called not to keep "bad company" but to live for the Lord in all that we do. We're cautioned against giving in to peer pressure and conforming to the world. At the same time, community is an essential part of being a believer. When we cultivate relationships with others who are walking along the same narrow path to salvation, we are forming a community that will lift us up and support us through all of our travels and trials.

As we walk down the path God has for us, there will be

times when we have a hard time seeing the Lord or knowing his will. But when we link arms with fellow believers and allow God into those relationships, we are forming a strong, unbreakable bond against the world's temptations. Fellow believers can also encourage and guide us when we become weary or confused.

We can take heart as we walk through this life and know that, though we may fall down, we have friends ready to pick us up, encourage us, and point us back to Jesus. And we can do the same for them.

The path that God has laid out for us might be difficult to find and even harder to stay on. The wide, welcoming path of the world might tempt us. But when we gather together with others to support each other on the journey, we're one step closer to our final destination.

Dear God, thank you for giving me a community of fellow believers who can help pick me up when I start to fall down. This road I'm walking isn't always an easy one, and I'm so grateful for the relationships—both with others and with you—that help me stay the course. Help me to be the same kind of support for others as they are for me. Amen.

....

Fill the box below with the names of your traveling companions—people who are there to help you up when you stumble and who encourage you in times of need. Then think about how you can do the same for them.

bonus adventure: entertainment itinerary

It's a challenge to find good and wholesome forms of entertainment that reflect our priorities and don't fill our minds with unhealthy thoughts. As Christians, it's important that we decide where we stand before temptations come along.

Let's explore the different entertainment options available to us as well as our own personal convictions, then formulate a go-to itinerary to make sure we don't end up wandering off the path.

HOW MUCH IS TOO MUCH?

- Am I comfortable reading or listening to content that contains bad language? How do I define bad language—coarse words, swear words, taking the name of the Lord in vain?

- When I'm reading or watching a love story, where do I draw the line? Am I keeping my mind pure when I'm engaging in these forms of entertainment?

- What are the messages conveyed in some of my favorite songs? Do I think about the lyrics? How does my favorite music make me feel? How does it affect my thoughts?

- Am I comfortable hanging out with friends whose boundaries are different from mine in these areas? How can I keep from engaging in activities I don't agree with and instead act as a good witness?

Did your answers to any of these questions surprise you? If so, consider adjusting your entertainment choices. If we don't have strong, firm guardrails in place to keep us from slipping into harmful decisions, it can be all too easy to find ourselves on the wrong path. Now that you've spent some time considering your own personal convictions, brainstorm some ways that you can have fun by yourself and with others while still holding your walk with the Lord above everything else.

CHAPTER 3

Goodbye, Baggage!

DAY 1: BAG DROP

READ PSALM 37:3-7

> *Delight yourself in the LORD; and He will give you*
> *the desires of your heart. ~ v. 4 (NASB)*

WHEN I PACK FOR A TRIP, I've been known to go a little over-board. It's just so hard to pare things down—who's to say I won't end up needing that extra pair of shoes?—and I always want to make sure I come prepared for some downtime with a book . . . or two or ten. More often than not, all of the extra things I throw in my suitcase at the last minute stay there until I'm back home. By that time, I've added a few pounds' worth of souvenirs to my already-hefty load, making my suitcase even harder to lug around than it was before.

I don't know about you, but I tend to do the same thing in life. I let my heart get cluttered with a lot of "baggage"—baggage that I don't want, don't need, and, more often than not, that just weighs me down as I walk the path God has planned for me. This baggage comes in a lot of different forms, many of which aren't inherently bad. There's nothing wrong with clinging tightly to treasured memories or being able to sing every song from your favorite album, but when we clutter our hearts and minds with "bad baggage"—negative thoughts toward ourselves and others, grudges, and everything else unpleasing to the Lord—well, that's when things get heavy.

But life doesn't have to be this way! In Christ, we have immense freedom—freedom to take that pesky, bothersome, encumbering baggage and drop it right at the feet of Jesus. All that junk in our lives and our hearts can take a while to work through, but our healing process can begin with a simple prayer.

In his Word, God tells us that *he* is the one who can give us the desires of our hearts. As we walk through this next chapter and discover more of the plans that God has for us, we're also going to learn how to discern which parts of our hearts are God-honoring and which would be better left behind on the baggage claim. God fills us—heart, soul, and mind—with hopes, dreams, desires, and goals that reflect his plans for our lives. How can we embrace any of that if our hearts are already filled to overflowing with stuff we don't need? Stuff that might be weighing us down more than we know?

God, my heart is full of wonderings and wishes, of past hurts and future hopes. Please show me more of what you want me to focus on. Help me to put my hope and trust in you, and help me to delight in your ways. Show me what you want from me, and fill my heart with your desires. Amen.

....

When do you find the most delight in your relationship with Christ? What parts of your heart's desires—your hopes and dreams and wonderings—might be coming directly from him? Write this chapter's key verse on a note card and stick it somewhere to remind yourself of God's blessings this week.

_____

_____

_____

_____

_____

_____

_____

_____

_____

DAY 2: BATTERED BOOTS

READ PSALM 51

> *Create in me a clean heart, O God,*
> *and renew a right spirit within me.* ~ *v. 10 (ESV)*

WHEN MY MOM AND I traveled to Europe, I brought along one of my favorite pairs of ankle booties. They were a light-tan color with a low heel—perfect for tromping around four different countries . . . or so I thought. Unfortunately, I hadn't realized quite how *much* tromping I would be doing . . . and I certainly hadn't expected them to get run over by my seventy-pound suitcase (while I was wearing them!) or drenched in not one or two but three major rainstorms. By the time I got back to the good old US of A, those shoes were toast. (My mom, on the other hand, brought a single pair of comfortable walking shoes that she still wears to this day. . . .)

This road that we call life is long and winding, full of twists and turns and spiritual mud puddles. Sometimes it feels like every bad choice or mistake we make results in our heart getting a little bit . . . grungier. We might wonder if God is going to discard us just like I said goodbye to my poor, battered booties.

But he doesn't!

Instead, God sees us and, despite our battered, bruised hearts, he *loves* us. Being the Master of mercy that he is, Jesus doesn't examine our flaws only to cast us aside. Instead, he takes our hearts, messy and imperfect though they are, and transforms them into a testament to his goodness.

Even when we make mistakes that we, as humans, find unforgivable, God is right there by our side. He's not going to throw us out or cast us away. Instead, he wants to heal us. Repair us. Give us a second chance—and a third and a fourth and so on—all the way to the end of our journey.

If your heart feels a little sullied and scratched today, turn to Jesus. He has the power and desire to turn all of your messed-up and broken parts into something beautiful. Something *new*.

Below, you'll find a chance to pray a prayer of salvation. If you've never trusted Jesus with your life, then now is the time to do so. Even if you've been a believer for a while now, there's nothing wrong with rededicating yourself to the Lord. Find a quiet space and take some time to bring yourself before the Lord today.

God, thank you for your love and mercy. I believe that you died on the cross and rose again three days later, defeating sin and death! Forgive me for the things I've done wrong, and please transform my heart into a new, clean creation so that I can serve you as I travel through this journey of life. Amen.

....

Congratulations! If you just prayed that prayer above, you are NEW in Christ! Your old struggles, problems, and regrets are now in the hands of the One who loves you most. Celebrate this new leg of your journey by listing some new, beautiful things—hopes, dreams, Scriptures to meditate on—that you'd like to fill your heart with in place of the old junk that you left behind with Jesus.

_____

_____

_____

_____

_____

_____

DAY 3: GHOST TOWN

READ EZEKIEL 36:24-38

> *I will put my Spirit in you*
> *and move you to follow my decrees. ~ v. 27*

ABOUT FORTY-FIVE MINUTES down the interstate from my house lies the little town of Golden. It's said that Golden was founded in the 1800s during the gold rush, and like many other mining towns of its time, its vivacity ran out along with the gold.

You can still visit the buildings, and weddings are even held in the church, which is on the National Register of Historic

Places, but no one lives in the town today. The gold is gone. If you visit late in the afternoon, stroll the empty footpaths, and listen to the wind whooshing through the broken windows of abandoned buildings, it's plain to see that Golden is a ghost town.

Today's passage in Ezekiel talks about a different type of ghost town. The Israelites' home—formerly a place of peace and prosperity—had fallen into ruin and desolation. The Israelites had turned away from their God and Father, and destruction had come upon them because of it. And yet, God remained faithful!

Through the prophet Ezekiel, God spoke promises of the restoration of the Israelites' former homeland . . . even though the Israelites didn't deserve it. Our God is a God of grace, one who wishes his name to be known throughout the world so that more people might come to know of his goodness. Even though the Israelites were in shambles, God promised to restore their land and, most importantly, redeem their souls.

Though the Israelites hauled around physical and spiritual baggage when they were in exile from the Promised Land, God had great compassion on them. He was willing to give them a second chance. In verse 26, he promised to cut out their cold, unfeeling, stone-heavy hearts and replace them with something softer. Something . . . *new*. And he's still doing the same thing today.

Golden never recovered after the gold ran out and the people living there moved on, but that's not how it works for God's people. Our God is a God of hope and renewal, and he wants to take our burdens and cleanse us from every sin, no matter what our past looks like. The ghost towns of our broken hearts don't have to stay sad and empty. In fact, they're ready and waiting to be filled with the love of the One who knows us best.

God, sometimes I feel like my future is a ghost town. Please forgive me for everything I've done wrong and restore my heart so that I can fully partake in all that you have planned for my life. Lead me and guide me even in my wilderness. Amen.

....

Do you feel lost or alone, like you're dragging around a bunch of baggage that you'd rather leave in God's hands? List your baggage here, pray over it, and release it into the hands of the One who knows you and loves you the most.

_____

_____

_____

_____

_____

_____

_____

_____

DAY 4: GIVE HIM YOUR BURDENS

READ MATTHEW 11:28-30

My burden is light. ~ v. 30

ONE TIME WHILE visiting Maui, my mom and I decided to head down to the beach. Since it was a nice day, I figured we'd want to stay awhile. I grabbed a portable camp chair from the closet in our condo, strapped it to my back, and took off.

After what felt like a mile or two of walking in the blazing-hot sun, we finally made it down the long, windy path from the condo to a secluded beach. True to my earlier estimation, I spent the rest of the afternoon on the beach—or, more accurately, floating with my mom in the bay. I barely sat on that chair for more than five minutes.

That extra baggage I'd brought with me to the beach was absolutely worthless. And then I had to lug it all the way back!

When we let our hearts get troubled by the wrong kind of baggage—thoughts, feelings, and fears that bring us more harm and frustration than good—we discover that we're easily exhausted, sick and tired of wasting so much mental energy on stuff that . . . well . . . just doesn't matter. Just like I was overprepared for the beach, we can tend to be overprepared in life, too. We spend so much time stressing about upcoming events, overanalyzing past conversations, and generally lugging a *bunch* of unnecessary baggage.

Instead of dragging around heavy issues that weigh down

our hearts and minds, let's start filling our days with thoughts of things that are *good*. As Christ's followers, we are called to fix our minds on things that bring him honor and glory. In doing that, though, we must first drop our cumbersome thoughts and feelings in the hands of the Lord.

In today's Bible passage, Jesus encouraged his followers to come to him with their burdens. In return, he promised them peace and rest for their souls—a promise that still holds true for us today.

Sometimes giving our burdens to Jesus can be hard to do—in some weird, wacky way it seems right to keep stressing and fretting over our internal baggage. We cling to old habits and thought patterns because they seem safe, almost comfortable. But we don't know what we're missing!

It is only when we exchange our heavy load for peace and joy in Jesus Christ that we truly understand the freedom that comes from living in him.

Jesus, I'm tired of carrying around my old hurts, past regrets, and new worries about the future. Today, I'm laying them all in your hands. Please restore my spirit and help me find peace and rest in your unfailing love. Amen.

....

Every time you find yourself trying to pick up that old, heavy baggage today, stop. Pray. Hand it back over to Jesus—as difficult as that may seem. Remind yourself that you are free in him, and walk in that freedom today!

DAY 5: WEIGHED DOWN

READ 2 CORINTHIANS 1:3-11

He will still deliver us. ~ v. 10 (NKJV)

HAVE YOU EVER tried to carry an enormous suitcase up and down multiple flights of stairs? While also racing to catch your one and only train to Rome? When you didn't speak a speck of Italian?

Probably not.

When I first went to Italy, my knowledge of the country's train system and language added up to about *nothing* . . . and I paid for my ignorance the day my mom and I took a train trip across the country. My physical burden was so heavy that I felt as though Paul's words in his second letter to the Corinthians were perfectly applicable—I "despaired of life itself"!

Okay, so I'm being overdramatic, but still.

In all seriousness, though, sometimes our burdens are so heavy that they weigh us down in every way possible. Our troubled memories and frantic worries about the future can combine in our hearts to bring us down . . . down . . . down.

Before we know it, we can be sinking in an emotional quicksand made of lies, fear, and sadness. When this happens, it's easy to lose faith in all that we know to be true—our own strength is often powerless against the monsters of fear, anxiety, and discouragement.

But that's where God comes in!

I had to struggle with my suitcase on my own that crazy day in Italy, but, thanks to Jesus' sacrifice for us on the cross, we don't have to get stuck in the thoughts and feelings that weigh us down. God has saved us not only from our sins but also from our worry and fear, our anxiety and sadness. No matter what's happened in our lives to weigh us down, God is walking right alongside us. His plans for us might include hard things, but because he's there, walking with us through them, we never need to be afraid. No matter what, our Lord will come alongside us and lift our burdens—one by one—so that we might once again walk in freedom.

Sometimes we just have to be brave enough to let go.

God, I want to stop living under the burdens of my past. Help me find your peace and rest as I give this baggage up to you. Amen.

....

What is weighing you down today? Write it here, and leave it here. Take today to clear your heart in preparation for filling it with the good things Christ has in store for you.

_____

_____

_____

_____

_____

DAY 6: LESSONS FROM LOCKDOWN

READ ROMANS 8:31-39

If God is for us, who can be against us? ~ v. 31

I'LL ALWAYS REMEMBER the day in the spring of 2020 when *coronavirus* became a regular part of my vocabulary. I remember how—almost overnight—my state shut down and even going to the grocery store was discouraged. I remember the widespread fear, the isolation, and the lack of toilet paper. (Really, will anyone ever forget the Great Toilet Paper Famine?)

I remember a lot from that crazy time, but one especially poignant memory is from the day I had to cancel my college graduation trip. My mom and I had spent weeks researching and dreaming about what we would do and see on our upcoming adventure, and the realization that our plans would never come to fruition was tough, to say the least.

In the middle of one of the most tumultuous years of my life—COVID notwithstanding—the dream of travel had become a sort of life preserver—a figment of normalcy to cling to when the entire world had been turned upside down. When even that was stripped away, it felt as if the last remaining pillar of my universe had come crashing down.

And yet.

That summer of 2020 turned out to be one of the best of my life. Instead of embarking on my long-awaited senior trip to explore the East Coast for the first time, I discovered that there was plenty of joy to be found right in my own backyard. I didn't have to travel somewhere new and exciting to celebrate God's blessings in my life; I simply had to open my eyes to the beauty all around me.

My mom and I researched recipes from every corner of the world and started having international-themed dinner nights out on our patio. We experimented with Moroccan stews, Japanese bento boxes, and Mexican street food. Blasting a playlist inspired by our country of choice and using a few knickknacks from around the house to decorate, we managed to create a new sort of travel experience. One that not even COVID could steal from us.

When I was at my weakest—when I was heavy and burdened and overwhelmed by the state of the world—the Lord stepped in. Even with a worldwide pandemic threatening to steal my health, happiness, and hope, God gave me the strength to put aside my worries and fears and enjoy simple, precious moments from his hand. Putting my trust in him and believing that everything would work out wasn't always easy, but as I continued to pray and seek him, I was able to rest in his plan, knowing he had everything under control. Looking back, I wouldn't trade a single day of that summer for anything—not even that trip to the East Coast.

Lord, sometimes all I can see are the parts of my life where things seem to be going wrong. Help me to spend more time with you and less time dwelling on my own problems. Take my worries for me today, and hold me close to your heart. Help me to walk the path you have for me, and give me hope even when I'm at my worst. Amen.

....

Have canceled plans or unexpected obstacles in your life become a burden? Write them down here—give them to God. Then spend some time praying about how God might use those trials and disappointments to lead you down a brighter path.

_____

_____

_____

_____

_____

_____

_____

_____

_____

_____

_____

_____

DAY 7: AN OVERFLOW OF LOVE

READ ROMANS 5:1-8

> *God's love has been poured out into our hearts.* ~ v. 5

HAVE YOU EVER walked beneath a waterfall? Behind a glimmering sheet of water, the outside world seems to twinkle and sparkle like a stained glass window. The rush of water pounding on the rocks below echoes in your ears; water droplets splatter on your face. Moss hangs from a rocky ceiling as you stare down . . . down . . . down at the river below.

Waterfalls are strong, powerful, and flat-out *amazing*. They keep entire rivers flowing just by filling them up. If a waterfall dries up, so does the riverbed beyond it. But there is one waterfall that will never run dry—the incredible flow of God's great love for his people.

The book of Romans tells us that God's love has been *poured* into our hearts—and that's not a little pitcher pour. It's a great big, raging, roaring, waterfall kind of pour. Close your eyes and picture Niagara Falls or Victoria Falls—or look up a photo of them. Then imagine yourself at the bottom of the falls, feeling that water pour over you. (Ignore the fact that you'd most likely drown.)

See, friends, God's love is raining down on us like that waterfall. But it isn't crushing us; it's *filling* us. The incredible outpouring of God's grace, mercy, and love goes straight to our hearts, overflowing them with joy and peace beyond measure.

The force of God's love for us—for *you*—is more powerful than any burden you might be carrying today. So why not surrender to the weight of his love and give your cares and worries to him? I know that can be hard to do. Sometimes it seems easier to cling to our problems, rolling them over and over in our minds in hopes of magically discovering the solution on our own. But why should we cling tightly to the baggage that weighs us down when we have a Savior ready and waiting to carry our load?

If you feel empty today—if you've been dragging your burdens behind you for too long and your heart is cracked and parched from walking through a spiritual wasteland—turn to Jesus. Let him shoulder your struggles, and rest beneath his waterfall of love and mercy. Look to him and be filled—be *renewed.*

God, thank you for the overwhelming outpouring of your love. Thank you for standing by me and carrying me even when I'm at my weakest. Encourage my heart today, take away my burdens, and fill me with your love. Amen.

....

If you can, visit a waterfall or small stream—if not, turn on a sink faucet and let the water run over your hands. Take a moment to be still and breathe, then imagine that the water flowing over you is a physical manifestation of God's love. Imagine it pouring over every part of you and filling your heart. Thank him for his love today.

DAY 8: PEDICAB PICKUP

READ PSALM 73:21-26

> *God is the strength of my heart . . . forever.* – v. 26

A FEW YEARS AGO, my mom and I took a weekend drive up the Columbia River Gorge. If you've ever visited this natural wonder—the river that separates my state of Oregon from Washington—you might be familiar with the windswept hills that rise up on either side of the gorge and the small, steeply sloped towns that border the river. I chose to explore one such town on a warm early summer day, and I spent the day wandering up and down the streets, climbing up staircases chiseled into the cliffs in order to get the best view of the gorge below.

And . . . wow. After a bunch of walking and hiking around the area, I was *exhausted*. Thankfully there was a pedicab company in town. Mom and I ended up riding around in one of those goofy-looking bicycle contraptions as our driver showed us around the rest of the town, eventually dropping us off at the small hamlet's most beloved ice cream parlor. *Yum!*

When my feet were worn and tired, it was such a relief to sink into the seat of that pedicab. What's even more of a relief is the knowledge that God is *always* with us and *always* ready to give us a reprieve from our burdens.

When we begin to feel like we can't possibly take another step, we have to remember this—we don't have to!

Our Lord has the strength to continually shoulder our

troubles and take care of them for us. As the psalmist writes, God is our eternal source of strength. Of life. Of *power*. He is walking with us, holding our hand, and giving us all that we need to make it through each day. The Lord is our everlasting protector—the One who loves us most.

Even at our emptiest, God can carry our heavy load. But we need to turn to him and fully rely on his ability to sustain us. That pedicab wasn't going to magically appear and offer me and my mom a free ride on a sticky June day—I had to flag it down. I had to jump in. I had to *ask*. When we open our hearts to the Lord and share our burdens with him, he is only too happy to give us the hope and help we need.

Really, the choice is up to us.

Dear God, thank you for guiding me down this long, winding path, and for giving me the strength to continue walking with you. Please carry me when I grow weary, and hold me tight as you show me your will for my life. Amen.

....

Do you need strength today? Why not take a long bubble bath or indulge in a special sweet treat while reading your Bible or listening to a favorite faith-based podcast? Sometimes all our hearts need for us to feel renewed is a little bit of rest!

DAY 9: THE FULLNESS OF GOD

READ EPHESIANS 3:14-21

> *Know this love that surpasses knowledge—that you may be*
> *filled to the measure of all the fullness of God. - v. 19*

EVERY TIME I say goodbye to someone, something, or somewhere special to me, I feel full. Okay, I also feel sad—really sad—but in the midst of the melancholy there's always this feeling of peace, of joy—of *fullness.*

I'll never forget the simultaneous tears in my eyes and joy in my heart as my mom and I drove back to the Kahului Airport in Maui after spending nearly two weeks on the enchanted island. Though I was disappointed to be saying goodbye to one of my favorite places in the world, I was also in awe of God's goodness. His power. His *might.* Not only had he blessed me with the opportunity to visit such a beautiful island, but he was the one who *made* it in the first place. God looked at that exact spot in the middle of the Pacific Ocean and thought, *I want to put an island there.* Did he do it simply for his own enjoyment? No! God did it for us, too. Our world is broken and sinful, yet God still chose to wave his paintbrush over every corner of the globe, filling it with natural wonders that whisper of his goodness.

I happen to feel the fullness of God most when I spend time in his creation, but really, we can be aware of his fullness at all times. Even when we're at our emptiest, we can be filled by the knowledge of his incredible, boundless love for us!

God's amazing natural creations pale in comparison to what his Son came to earth to do. Jesus didn't come here just to spend time with us or to soak in the beauty of his Father's creation. He came to defeat death and demonstrate his glorious love for us. His sacrifice on the cross perfectly exemplifies the knowledge-surpassing love that the apostle Paul wrote of in today's reading.

When our hearts are heavy laden and burdened, or when we feel empty inside, we can run to Jesus. It's easy to forget exactly what he went through on the cross to bring us eternal life, but when we take a step back and think about it . . . wow. *Wow!*

Just like I feel awed by and filled with God's power and majesty when I experience the vastness of creation, we can be filled at any moment of the day when we meditate on "the breadth and length and height and depth" (3:18, ESV) of his great love.

God, I'm so grateful for your love. Even when I am at my weakest, you are making me strong! Help me to grow in you and know your love more and more. Fill me up with you, Lord. Amen.

As you go throughout your day, be on the lookout for moments that make you feel full. Hold tightly to them—maybe even write about them in a journal—and consider how you can use those moments to grow even closer to your Creator.

DAY 10: PACK WISELY

READ PHILIPPIANS 4:4-8

> *Whatever is true, whatever is noble, whatever is right, whatever is pure, whatever is lovely, whatever is admirable—if anything is excellent or praiseworthy—think about such things. ~ v. 8*

PICTURE THIS: you're standing in an alpine meadow. All around you, wildflowers wave in the breeze. A crystal-clear brook babbles as it runs parallel to the path you're on. Craggy, snow-dusted mountains tower around you on every side. The sky is your favorite shade of blue.

Wiggle your toes—feel the soft grass underneath. Breathe in deep—catch the sharp, silvery scent of snow from the mountains beyond. Listen closely—can you hear the distant lowing of cattle and the jangle of sheep bells?

Okay, so maybe the sound of cattle is actually your dog snoring on the ground beneath your feet, or that jingle-jangle of sheep bells is actually silverware clinking on the dining room table. Imaginary vacations only last so long.

Now that we're back from our trip to that peaceful bit of Alpine bliss, what have you been thinking about? Was your imagination strong enough to block out life's distractions and mentally transport you to the spot I just described, or did you struggle to put aside everything that's running through your mind and fully immerse yourself in the experience?

I know that, for me, it can be *really* hard to let go of all the negative stuff I'm clinging to and give it up to God. Fears, worries, and concerns become my traveling companions far more often than I'd like. And that's wrong! In fact, in God's Word, he commands us to stop living in a cycle of negative thought.

God wants to take us to a place of peace and rest, of joy and gladness. One day we'll be there for real, when Jesus returns. Until that time comes, though, God has other things in store for us—and none of them include dragging around bags packed with regrets, anxieties, or worries.

Just like I encouraged you to take a mental vacation to a beautiful alpine field, God wants us to take a different kind of trip. He's inviting us to unpack our suitcases of doubt and dissatisfaction and, instead, to pack our minds with *good things*.

Our Father gives us good gifts, and when we fill our minds with praise and gratitude, we are not only setting ourselves up for a better day—we're also honoring him.

Dear God, sometimes it's hard for me to dwell on good things. Help me to guard my thoughts and my heart and to focus more on the blessings that you've given me. Amen.

....

Read today's verse several times throughout the day and ask yourself how you can discipline your thoughts in the way Paul encourages us to do.

bonus adventure: baggage claim or lost luggage?

What is on your mind most often? Sometimes we spend way too much time carting around discouraging thoughts and emotional baggage that should really get lost so we can claim God's promises and use them to fuel our hearts and minds. The following space is for you to explore the baggage claim of your mind. What thoughts would you rather lose? What do you want to replace them with? Write down toxic thoughts that you need to do away with. Then spend some time thinking of God-honoring topics and truths that you can dwell on instead of negative thought patterns.

GET-LOST THOUGHTS:

_____

_____

_____

_____

_____

_____

_____

BETTER BAGGAGE TO CLAIM:

_____

_____

_____

_____

_____

_____

If you're struggling to unpack your mind's baggage and replace negative thoughts with those that are honoring to God, know that you're not alone! We all struggle sometimes to leave anxious feelings or painful memories behind. When it's hard to release our hold on old, toxic ways of thinking, we have to trust in the Lord, meditate on his Word, and remind ourselves that his promises are real and true and *beautiful*. It's not always easy, but the more we fix our minds on things from above instead of our own worries and troubles, the more we will find that God's grace is sufficient to cover our entire life.

CHAPTER 4

Trust the Guide

DAY 1: INVISIBLE GUIDE

READ 1 CORINTHIANS 6:12-20

Whoever is united with the Lord is one with him in spirit. ~ v. 17

IMAGINE YOU'RE ON vacation in Maui and your parents sprang for tickets for the entire family to take a bus tour down the Road to Hana. (If you're not familiar with this famously winding road, google it real quick to get an idea of just how frightening it is. Don't worry—I'll wait.) You show up the morning of the tour and board an old, rickety minibus. The driver leans against the hodgepodge of duct-taped metal and smiles at you as you hop aboard. You do your best to smile back, even though you're 99 percent sure you're going to be sick during some portion of the trip or another.

"Don't be afraid." The driver claps you on the back and smiles. "I've driven this road a million times. I know it like the back of my hand." He holds up a hand as if for emphasis, but it seems to shimmer—disappear, really—in the pale morning sunshine.

You shrug and climb aboard with the rest of your family, but the driver never gets in the driver's seat. After a few minutes, you peek out the bus window, but you can't see him outside, either.

He's vanished!

And then suddenly the bus starts—by itself. Like magic.

"Hang on tight! It's gonna get a little bumpy." That's the driver's voice—but where *is* he? The bus starts moving all on its own, the steering wheel twisting and turning at just the right moments to keep you and your family from flying off a cliff and into the churning Pacific Ocean below.

Your driver is invisible.

Just like it would be terrifying to take a trip with the driver from the story above, it can feel frightening to set off on this adventure called life when our guiding Savior isn't visible to us. We know God has a plan for us—a road map for our life. We know he's always with us. We know he'll guide us toward our dreams and goals when we delight ourselves in him. But how can we truly get to know him when he's not . . . you know . . . physically *here*?

Though today's passage mostly focuses on the importance of staying away from sexual immorality, it also holds some important truths about Christ that can help us in other parts of our lives. For example, this chapter's key verse reveals to us that, as God's chosen people, we are united with him. That means that, even though we can't hear, see, or touch the Lord, he is closer to us than the clothes on our body or the shoes on our feet. His Spirit is *in* us.

Jesus isn't an invisible tour guide who's all talk and no show—he's a living, breathing, *loving* God. We might not be able to see him in the flesh, but we can know through the promises in his Word that we are loved, chosen, and called by him to walk down the path he has for us.

And rain or shine, good or bad, he is with us.

Dear God, when life gets tough and the path you've laid out for me starts to twist and turn, it can be hard to believe that you're really here. Thank you for living in me and not forsaking me. Help me to remember that, even when I don't feel your presence, you are still near. Amen.

....

Have you had an experience with Jesus that reminds you of today's opening story? Has he taken the wheel of your life and brought you through something that seemed impossible? How could you feel his presence during that time? (And don't forget to copy down this chapter's key verse on a note card or add it as a reminder on your phone!)

_____

_____

_____

_____

_____

_____

DAY 2: ALWAYS NEAR

READ ACTS 17:24-28

He is not far from any one of us. – v. 27

—◦○◦—

WHEN MY MOM took me to Seattle for the first time, we were excited to stay at a fancy hotel downtown. Not only did we have a view of the Space Needle, but we were also close to downtown and some of the best department stores. Except . . . we weren't exactly sure how to get there! (Yes, this was before we got phones with built-in GPS.)

We finally found our way to the shopping district and spent hours window-shopping until we were ready to drop. But first we had to locate the hotel. It took us one hour plus a million wrong turns to find it. When we finally arrived, we realized that the very store we'd been unable to get back from was on the same street as the hotel! (Can you guess that our sense of direction is about zero? In fact, we ended up getting lost *again* that very night . . . we're talented like that.)

Just like our hotel ended up being about as close as you

could get to that department store, God is so much closer to our hearts than we could ever imagine.

Even when we feel far from God, he is right beside us. The Lord will never forsake us, but sometimes he doesn't make himself known right away. It's not because he doesn't care—it's because sometimes he wants us to first seek him. When we quiet our souls and are still—when we search for the Lord and listen for his voice—that is often when we truly hear him.

Do you feel like you're walking in circles today—that you can't seem to find the one your soul is searching for? We've all been there. (I, in fact, am in that place as I write these words.) Let's take today to truly seek after Jesus. Let's reach out for him—he's nearer than we could ever even imagine.

Dear God, thank you for never leaving my side, even when life is overwhelming. I'm so thankful that you're never far away and that your plan for my life is always bigger, better, and more beautiful than anything I could come up with for myself. Please draw near to me today, Lord, and guide me. Amen.

....

Have you listened to the song "Way Maker"? Even if you've heard it a bunch of times or sung it at church, give it another listen—and pay close attention to the lyrics. Which ones stand out most to you today?

_____

_____

_____

_____

_____

_____

DAY 3: HE WELCOMES US

READ HEBREWS 10:19-23

Draw near to God with a sincere heart. ~ v. 22

──◦◦◦──

WHENEVER I TRAVEL somewhere new—whether it's a city in a
foreign country or a town in a neighboring county—I love to
wander around with family and friends and discover where the
locals live. We usually start down narrow, crowded alleyways
and keep walking until we've reached a fancier, more exclusive
part of town. There's something about gazing at luxurious,
opulent homes that takes my breath away. I love to stare at the
perfectly manicured front yards and imposing double doors
and try to picture the beauty that must lie inside.

But, at the same time, I know I'm not welcome there.

I can imagine that what I feel when I stand on the sidewalk
in front of these magnificent, impenetrable houses must be a
dim reflection of the way God's people felt before Jesus sacrificed his life. See, the Most Holy Place (or Holy of Holies)
had long been forbidden to most of the Israelites—a place

so sacred that only the high priest could enter it once a year. It was, after all, the room where the very presence of God dwelled. But then Jesus came down to the earth, taking our sins upon his shoulders and making a way for humans to come to God. When Jesus died on the cross, something strange and miraculous happened. The veil that separated the Most Holy Place from the rest of the Temple split in two.

No longer must we rely on a high priest when we wish to communicate with our Lord. Thanks to the mighty work Jesus did on the cross, God now dwells in the hearts of his children. Jesus *is* our high priest! If we are living lives devoted and committed to him, then he lives in us. No longer are we standing on the outside, separate from God's love. When we accept Christ's gift of eternal life, we are opening our hearts to the Lord's amazing grace, forgiveness, and mercy. We are *saved*.

But, dear friends, we are so much more than saved. We are cleansed. Our hearts have been purified. Our very bodies have become the only temple that the Holy Spirit needs. He loves *us* and lives in *us*. We're no longer on the outside looking in—we are welcomed in by *the One*. What an amazing gift, indeed.

Lord, thank you for coming to the earth to die for my sins and for dwelling in my heart by your Spirit. Thank you for your mercy and goodness, and for your love for me. Make my heart into a place worthy of your presence. Amen.

Read about the Tabernacle in Exodus 26, focusing especially on verses 31-34, and envision what the Most Holy

Place must have looked like. The Lord once dwelled among his people in a skillfully crafted tent, but now he lives in you! Is your heart an acceptable dwelling place for Jesus? What parts of your heart honor him and bring him glory, and which parts might you still need to surrender to him?

_____

_____

_____

_____

_____

_____

_____

DAY 4: LOST IN THE CROWD

READ ROMANS 8:35-39

Who shall separate us from the love of Christ? ~ v. 35

THE FIRST TIME I went to Disneyland, I was in for a complete sensory overload. My favorite movie characters paraded around in real life, thrilling rides beckoned, and there was more *food* than four-year-old me could've dreamed of.

As usual, I allowed myself to get completely distracted by said food one morning at a bottomless buffet. Between the sight of a giant stack of donuts and a platter of Mickey-shaped waffles, I couldn't manage to keep my eyes fixed on my parents. By the time I finished ogling the vast array of sugary breakfast goodies and turned around, my mom and dad were gone!

I ran frantically through the restaurant, searching for a familiar face—and then I found one.

Piglet.

Yes, the sweet, lovable pink pig from *Winnie-the-Pooh* found me in my time of need and reunited me with my parents. What had started out as my worst nightmare ended in a photo for the memory books—and a couple of those mouse-shaped waffles, too. Being reunited had never felt so good.

Sometimes, though, I still feel like that scared four-year-old girl. I might not be dodging strangers in a crowded, unfamiliar restaurant, but I *do* fight against fear and worry as I walk down the path God has for me. When life gets crazy and we take our eyes off Jesus, it's easy to feel lost.

As Paul wrote, though, there is nothing in this world that can separate us from the incredibly powerful, fierce, and *real* love of Christ Jesus. The devil might try to pull us off the path God has for us—sometimes he might even succeed. But even when we get lost, God is still there. Watching out for us. Loving us. Guiding us back to his path.

If you feel lost today, let this be your reminder that you are not alone. No matter what you're walking through, you can find peace in the knowledge that God is walking with you.

Nothing will make him stop loving you. He lives in us, and he loves us. He never fails.

Dear God, thank you for never leaving my side. Help me to find the path you want me to walk, and help me keep my eyes on you as I seek your will for my life.

....

Get lost! Take a walk and don't think about where you'll end up. (Well, think about it a little bit—or at least let someone know what you're doing so no one files a missing person report while you're gone.) When you start to get tired, stop and sit down on the first bench you see. Spend some time alone with the Lord, soaking in his presence.

DAY 5: GUIDANCE FROM THE SPIRIT

READ ISAIAH 11:1-5

> *The Spirit of the LORD will rest on him—the Spirit of wisdom and of understanding, the Spirit of counsel and of might, the Spirit of the knowledge and fear of the LORD. ~ v. 2*

I DON'T KNOW about you, but I do a lot of dumb things when I'm traveling. There's something about being away from home, out of my normal routine, that causes the wires in my brain to short-circuit. Before I know it, I'm plugging my high-speed hair dryer into a European power socket (bad idea) or taking a fourteen-mile walk in heels (even worse idea).

Let's just say that I don't always make the wisest choices on vacation—and I've been known to make some bad decisions in my personal life too. When I forget to ask the Lord to guide and direct me, things . . . don't go all that well. On the contrary, when I remember to turn to Jesus and give him complete authority over my life—well, that's totally different.

And that's why we need the Holy Spirit. Like, all the time. He is the one and only voice of true wisdom—the only One who knows and understands our own hearts even better than we do. Today's passage is a prophecy about how God would send his Spirit to help our eternal Savior, Jesus—but there's more to it than that. Think about it—that same Spirit who rested on Jesus and guided him through life on this earth comes to lives in us when we repent and trust in him.

Read that again.

The very same Spirit who lived in Jesus is alive today, guiding the hearts and minds of his people. The same God who gave Christ the strength to sacrifice his life is giving us strength too. As we walk down the path that the Lord has laid out for us, the Holy Spirit is living in us and directing us, just like he did for Jesus. Wow.

God isn't just "the big man in the sky." Jesus was more than a good man. And the Holy Spirit is still alive and active in each of our lives today. Together, all three members of the Trinity are working in our lives, comforting us as we need it, and leading the way for us as we walk down the path that the Lord has for us.

Dear heavenly Father, thank you for being real—for being here. Thank you for sending your Son to die for us and for giving us the gift of your Holy Spirit. Please open my heart to hear and understand your guiding Word. Amen.

....

As believers, we are all children of the same God who called Jesus his Son! How does it feel to know that the very Father that Jesus called upon in the Bible is looking after you—and that the same Holy Spirit that Jesus sent to his disciples is the one who's living within you, too?

_____

_____

_____

_____

_____

_____

_____

_____

_____

_____

DAY 6: A GALAXY OF LIGHT

READ PSALM 23

> *Even though I walk through the darkest valley,*
> *I will fear no evil, for you are with me. ~ v. 4*

HAVE YOU EVER been somewhere where there was no light? Literally *no light*?

The last time my mom and I visited the Oregon coast, we stayed in a condo just across from the ocean. One night, I woke up around three in the morning and, just out of curiosity, decided to step out onto my balcony. The brisk coastal air greeted me, and I wrapped my arms around myself for want of a sweater. It was pitch-black outside. Though there were a few other houses up and down the road, there were no streetlights to be seen.

It was only then—in the dark, still night with the echo of waves from the shore pounding in my ears—that I thought to look up. And *that* is where the light was.

That night, shivering on a balcony high above the waves, I saw the true glory of the heavens like never before. Gone was the modest handful of stars that I'd grown used to seeing from my bedroom window at home. In their place was an entire galaxy of light—of *life*. There was more light in the sky than there was darkness that night, and it made me tremble at the complete and total amazingness of our Creator.

It was also a beautiful and timely reminder that, even in the darkness of this world, there is always light—and that Light is Christ. God loves us more than words can express. Our Father's love knows no bounds.

Just like that starry sky stretched far beyond what the eye could see, God's love for us is never-ending. Even when we're walking through the darkest night of our souls, we can take heart and find comfort because he is with us.

And when I say that God is with us, I don't just mean that he's hovering above our heads some million miles away in heaven. I mean he's really *with* us—in our hearts, in our souls. He's walking alongside us, holding our hand or even carrying us when we need it. The Lord has not left us to walk through this life alone. He's here with each of us. Every single second. Every day. Forever.

Dear God, thank you for never leaving me. Thank you for walking with me as I pass through the darkest, most frightening valleys. Please make your presence known to me today, and help me to live my life in a way that will make you proud. Amen.

....

Stay up late—or get up early—and admire the stars. Even in the middle of the night, the stars shine brightly. So, too, does the love of God shine in the midst of darkness.

DAY 7: THE SPIRIT OF TRUTH

READ JOHN 16:12-15

> *When he, the Spirit of truth, comes,*
> *he will guide you into all the truth.* ~ v. 13

WHEN MY MOM took me on my "trip-of-a-lifetime" cruise around Europe, we met some seriously wonderful people. Two of them, though—our dinner partners—stand out. Over the course of the trip, the four of us became incredibly close. I even came to think of them as my "cruise grandparents." They knew *everything*! I'm forever grateful to them for completely rescuing me from what was sure to be a tourist-trap nightmare on my first day in Italy.

Since they'd been to Europe several times before, they were far more experienced than I was. They were able to help me turn what was sure to be a disastrous excursion into the busy, crowded, disorienting city center of Naples into a dreamy day on the Italian isle of Capri.

Without my cruise grandparents as my guide, I would've been in for a hot, sticky, and somewhat miserable day—and *that's* assuming I didn't get run over by a moped first!

Just like this kind older couple came alongside me and helped me learn the basics of European tourism, we, too, have a Helper—a heavenly tour guide who is ready and waiting to lead us down the right path.

When Jesus was preparing to depart from earth and return to his Father in heaven, he promised his disciples that he would leave them a Guide. That Guide is the same Spirit who lives in each of our hearts today when we trust in Christ.

In the Bible, Jesus says that this Holy Spirit is a Spirit of truth and glory. He speaks only that which comes from above, and he is living within us—leading us, loving us, and directing us down the right path.

We could all use some truth, guidance, or direction today, couldn't we? So often, when we're in need of a dose of wisdom, it's easy to look outward, trusting whatever the world promises will show us the way. What if, today, we stopped tuning in to outward distractions? What if, instead, we turned inward? What if we inclined our ear to God's Word before listening to the clamor of the world?

When we do this, we're not just bringing glory and honor to our heavenly Father. We're also giving ourselves every opportunity to have a meaningful and joy-filled trip along the path he has laid out for us.

Dear Lord Jesus, thank you for sending your Holy Spirit to minister to us. Help me to listen to your voice and trust your counsel as I explore all that this life has to offer. Amen.

....

The Sprit of truth lives in you! Think about how that makes you feel. Then use your own words to fill out the acrostic poem below to reflect those feelings. (The first letter is done for you.)

T rusting that God's plans for my heart are better
   than my own

R _____

U _____

T _____

H _____

DAY 8: HOME SWEET HOME

READ 1 JOHN 4:16-19

> *God is love, and whoever abides in love abides in God,*
> *and God abides in him. ~ v. 16 (ESV)*

AS MUCH AS I LOVE traveling to new and unusual locations
and staying in quirky hotels, exciting resorts, or cozy cottages,
I'll always have one favorite destination—*home.* No matter
where I go or what sort of wonders I see, I have to admit
there's something about my hometown, my neighborhood,
and even my own backyard that speaks to my soul like nothing else.

Similarly, we will journey through many troubles and
heartaches over the course of this crazy life, but take heart—
we can always come home to our true and loving Savior. Just
like there's something special about returning home after a

long, hard day, there's something even more precious about being able to come to Jesus and fall on his grace in the midst of our trials.

In 1 John, the author tells us that God is *love*. When we abide in God—when we live in him and let him work through us—we are actually opening ourselves up to him and giving him total access to our hearts.

Sometimes it's easy to focus so much on God's justice that we lose sight of the fact that he is also a God of love. When Jesus Christ dwells in us by his Spirit, he's not simply keeping watch over us to make sure we don't mess up (though he certainly doesn't want us to, and he helps us resist temptation), but he's also holding us securely. His love and care are unrivaled by anything else in this world. Because God is at work in us, we can be full of love—living it, breathing it, and showing it to everyone around us.

Not only do we serve a God who lives in us, but we also serve a God who loves us. His presence is the very essence of love—a kind of love so deep and precious that we can find our home in it. What a powerful gift that is!

Dear Lord, sometimes it's easy to forget who you are—the God of love. Remind me of your grace and goodness today, and help me live a life worthy of the kind of love you give. Amen.

....

What is one thing you can do today to show Christ's love to others? Write it down here, then go do it!

_____

_____

_____

DAY 9: A GLORIOUS GARDEN

READ JEREMIAH 17:9-11

I the LORD search the heart. ~ v. 10

PICTURE THIS: You wake up in paradise. To your right is a beautiful garden filled with more flowers and fruit trees than you ever could have envisioned. Above you lies a cloudless, crystalline sky the color of the sea. Beneath you is a grassy meadow—not the kind of grass that's prickly and poky, but soft, sweet-smelling, verdant grass. The slight breeze is rich with the scent of lilacs, and the temperature outside is *just right.*

Have you guessed where you are? If you think this heavenly oasis sounds like the Garden of Eden, then you're exactly right.

Of course, no one knows exactly what this Christ-designed garden actually looked like, but it sure is fun to imagine, isn't it?

You're probably familiar with the story of all that happened in the Garden of Eden (if you're not, read Genesis 3 to refresh your memory), but what I want to touch on today is God's incredible omnipotence. Hebrews 4:13 tells us that God sees all and knows all. That means he knew of Adam and Eve's sin even before he questioned them in the Garden.

The Lord searches each of our hearts and knows them completely, the same way he knew about Adam and Eve's fall before they confessed their sins to him.

That thought is a little scary. The realization that God knows every part of us—heart, soul, and mind—can be overwhelming. But God doesn't become so intimately acquainted with us because he wants to condemn us. He lives in us because he *cares* for us.

Think about it. Any mistakes you've made are already known by the Lord—even if you're too ashamed to admit them aloud. God knows every facet of our hearts, every aspect of our being, and he chooses to love us anyway. Even though our hearts start out deceitful and unwise, the Lord is still willing to make his dwelling place there. And, as he lives there, he begins to transform and sanctify us so that we look more and more like him.

Adam and Eve's sin might have cost us a life spent in paradise, but we still have access to the greatest gift we could ever ask for—complete and total fellowship in our hearts with Christ through his Holy Spirit. And that is far better than a garden oasis.

Dear Lord, what an honor it is to know that you see every part of me—and still choose to love me. Thank you for your loving-kindness, your grace and forgiveness. Please, Lord, search my heart and show me my weaknesses so that I might grow in love and trust in you.

What does your heart look like today? What might Christ see in there? In the heart-shaped box below, write down what's burdening you right now. Don't be afraid to put it out in the open—after all, the Lord already knows your whole heart backward and forward.

DAY 10: WHEREVER WE GO

READ PSALM 139:1-12

Your right hand will hold me fast. – v. 10

THE WORLD is a big, big place—and that's an understatement.

It would take us more than seventeen days to drive around the earth's circumference without stopping to get food, fill up on gas, or take a bathroom break. Talk about a *looooong* road trip! (Which is unfortunate because I'd give anything to hop in the car and take a drive to the Maldives. Or Morocco. Or Moscow. Or anywhere else, basically.)

And yet, despite the utter vastness of this world, the psalmist writes that the presence of the Lord would be with us even if we were to move to the far side of the sea or the depths of the earth.

Wow.

No matter where we go, we are never apart from God. (Check out the story of Jonah if you need to be reminded of this!) When we trust in him, the Lord is alive and active in our hearts, every second of every day. And today's passage makes it clear that Christ isn't just along for the ride. No, he's working in us, watching over us, and caring deeply for us. He knows our innermost thoughts. He follows our every step. He has his hand over every aspect of our lives.

Of course, that won't always prevent bad things from happening—we live in a fallen and sinful world. But with the love of Christ at work in our hearts and in our lives, we can stand strong and walk in the assurance that he is always there.

That's a beautiful thought, isn't it? However, sometimes it's easy to forget all of that—I know it's happened to me. For whatever reason, I've decided to ditch my heavenly tour guide and go blaze my own trails far more times than I'd care to admit.

But, in all honesty, don't we all?

Just like Jonah jumped ship (literally) and tried to pretend *he* knew better than the Lord, I know I've done the same thing in my own life—minus the giant fish, thank goodness. Let's face it—humans are a stubborn breed. We like to think that we have our lives perfectly planned out. Sometimes, especially when God's plan seems vague or frightening, it seems easier to go our own way. Jonah's disobedience resulted in an unplanned detour to the belly of a fish, and we find ourselves in trouble more often than not when we deviate from God's path.

That's why it's so, so important for us to remember that the Lord is always with us. And not only that—His plans for us are greater and more powerful than anything we could imagine. So let's hold on. Trust the Guide and listen to his voice. The road may be bumpy, but our Savior is by our side. Today, tomorrow, and through all eternity.

Dear Lord Jesus, thank you for being here—with me. Right here. Right now. Please open my eyes and my heart so that I might experience more of your presence. Guide me today, Lord, I pray. Amen.

Keep an eye out for any uncanny coincidences (aka "God things," like a Bible verse that keeps popping up in different places) that reveal the Lord's presence during your day. Then write about them here!

_____

_____

_____

_____

_____

_____

_____

bonus adventure: one-on-one

This extra-special adventure was designed just for you—and the Lord. Set aside some time this weekend to make a cup of this south-of-the-border hot chocolate and work through the following journaling questions. Make sure you're in a cozy and quiet space, and play some soft instrumental music to help you focus as you draw nearer to the Lord through this time of fellowship with him.

Mexican Spiced Hot Chocolate

1 CUP MILK

2 TABLESPOONS CHOCOLATE CHIPS (Feel free to sub white
chocolate if that's more your thing.)

1 TABLESPOON BROWN SUGAR

½ TEASPOON VANILLA

A PINCH OF SALT (or more, if you, like me, are a fan of salty/sweet)

CINNAMON AND CAYENNE PEPPER (to taste)

WHIPPED CREAM

MARSHMALLOWS

A CINNAMON STICK (optional, for stirring)

Heat the milk in the microwave or on a stovetop until it
is steaming but not quite boiling. Add the chocolate, brown
sugar, vanilla, spices, and salt, and stir for about thirty seconds
or until the chocolate melts. Top with whipped cream and
marshmallows, plus an extra sprinkle of cinnamon and a cinnamon stick for stirring. Enjoy!

JOURNALING QUESTIONS

- Do I find it easy to trust God, myself, and others,
  or do I struggle to give up control? When is it most
  difficult to place my trust in the Lord?

- Has there been a time in my life when I was able to totally let go of my fears and trust God? What was that like?

- What am I holding on to right now that I wish I could hand over to God? Why haven't I been able to release that part of my life?

- Who, out of all my friends and family members, do I trust the most? How might this person be able to help me as I work to place more of my trust in the Lord?

- What verse from this chapter especially stood out to me? (Consider memorizing it to help you when you're struggling to trust God.)

CHAPTER 5

Bumps in the Road

DAY 1: ANXIOUS FOR NOTHING

READ PHILIPPIANS 4:1-7

*Be anxious for nothing, but in everything by prayer
and supplication, with thanksgiving, let your requests
be made known to God; and the peace of God,
which surpasses all understanding, will guard your
hearts and minds through Christ Jesus. – vv. 6-7 (NKJV)*

YOU'RE LYING IN BED, wide awake. Thoughts whiz through your head almost faster than you can think them. Your room is cozy and dark, save for maybe the slight glow of a streetlamp beyond the window. You might even be listening to relaxing music or have lavender-scented lotion on your hands. But, no matter what, you can't sleep.

Sound familiar?

I feel exactly like this the night before I leave on a trip, whether it's an around-the-world adventure, a weekend getaway, or even a long-awaited day trip. It's called being *excited*! I never sleep well the night before a vacation because I can hardly wait to jet out the front door the next morning and start exploring somewhere exotic and thrilling or familiar and welcoming.

Unfortunately, excitement and anxiety are close cousins. In fact, the feeling of anxiety is frighteningly similar to that wide-eyed, heart-pounding exhilaration that keeps us on pins and needles before a trip. Just replace said exhilaration with apprehension and you're halfway to the panic attack of the century. As someone who struggles with anxiety, I know the feeling all too well.

That's why this chapter's key verse is so incredible! Seriously, go read Philippians 4:6-7 again.

There is nothing on this earth that needs to cause us anxiety because, when we go to the Lord in prayer, thanking him for his good works and asking him for help, he will give us the sort of peace that goes beyond the sublunary to the supernatural. Through God's great work, this serenity that he gives us keeps our hearts and minds safe. From *anything*.

We all go through turbulence in our lives and experience things that cause us anxiety. Sometimes this turbulence takes the form of a bump here and there; other times it seems to come over us all at once, jostling our hearts and minds and emotions until we hardly know which way is up. But even when we encounter these disconcerting seasons in our lives, God is our ultimate Navigator. He's always in control. With Jesus Christ as our tour guide, traveling companion, and pilot, we truly can be anxious for nothing. He is holding us in the palm of his huge, holy, mighty hand. And *he* is keeping us safe.

Dear Lord Jesus, sometimes this life is frightening. I feel like I'm getting bumped around and banged up and bruised. My mind is racing, and I just can't get it to stop. Will you give me your peace today? Quiet my heart and mind and help me to see you amid my anxiety. Amen.

....

What is something you're feeling anxious about right this second? Write it down here, then pen a short prayer, thanking God for one special blessing in your life and asking him for help conquering your anxiety. Then copy down this chapter's key verse separately so you can memorize these life-giving words!

_____

_____

_____

_____

_____

_____

DAY 2: CARED FOR AND COMFORTED

READ 1 PETER 5:6-11

Cast all your anxiety on him because he cares for you. ~ v. 7

ONE YEAR WHEN I WAS LITTLE, my mom sprang for a Christmastime girls' getaway to a historic inn nestled in the mountains outside of town. When we arrived, there was a slight dusting of snow on the ground—nothing to get excited over. But, before we went to bed that night, something magical happened. It started snowing. Hard.

By the time we woke up the next morning, the quiet mountain town had been transformed into a winter wonderland. Of course, I wanted to go outside and play! I threw snowballs, made snow angels, and even constructed a fairly impressive snowman (with a pine cone for a nose, since I hadn't been prudent enough to pack a carrot in my suitcase). But by the time I was finished, I was a living, walking icicle.

Thank goodness for the innkeeper, who ushered my mom and me into the dining room and proceeded to cook us a massive breakfast complete with frothy hot chocolate and fresh-baked croissants. All these years later, I can still remember just how delicious everything tasted on that chilly morning. The kindness and care that the innkeeper showed us that day has never left my heart.

It's a special thing—to be cared for. A single kind word or gesture from a friend, parent, or other loved one can turn even the worst day ever into something beautiful. How much more, then, does our Lord care for us? Not only does he love us completely and unconditionally, but he also desires to "lift us up"—honor us—when the time is right (1 Peter 5:6).

Really, Christ's love and care for us have many things in common with the attention to detail exhibited by the staff at that inn in the mountains. Our heavenly Father is constantly watching out for us, loving us, and giving us good gifts. Even more than that, he wants to carry our burdens. Whether we're sick, hurting, or struggling, God is with us. Comforting us through it all.

This is especially true when we're struggling with anxiety. Sometimes Jesus is the only One who can fully take our fears from us. How does he do this? It surely isn't a one-time, split-second action. Instead, it often happens gradually—it's hard for us to completely surrender our worries and fears! Eventually, though, we can get to the point where the fears and worries that once plagued us are no longer so distressing. So how can we start this anxiety-easing process?

The book of 1 Peter gives us the answer. We are to *cast* our anxieties upon the Lord. That means bringing our concerns to him in prayer—not as a last resort, but as the first line of defense. Of course, this is easier to do in theory than it is in real life. With our hectic schedules and day-to-day stressors, it can be difficult for us to remember to seek God first when things get crazy. But the more we practice bringing our concerns to him first and foremost, the more it will become second nature.

Friends, whatever you're facing today, I hope and pray that

you will cast all of your burdens upon the Lord. He loves you deeply and is fully capable of carrying that heavy load.

Dear God, it's so easy for me to let my thoughts run away when worries and fears crop up. Please help me to come to you first and leave my anxieties in your loving and capable hands. Amen.

How can you remember to bring your anxieties to the Lord first, before letting them obliterate the rest of your brain? Use this space as a "brain dump" for the day, and write down whatever might be troubling you.

_____

_____

_____

_____

_____

_____

_____

_____

_____

_____

DAY 3: CALL ON HIM

READ JAMES 5:13-18

The prayer of a righteous person is powerful and effective. – v. 16

LIVING IN THE GORGEOUS PNW, I'm blessed to be surrounded by natural beauty on every side. A ride in the car with a friend can take me to the coast, the mountains, the lake—you name it, Oregon has it! However, these car trips often lead us down narrow, winding two-lane roads in the middle of nowhere. There are few signs of civilization, let alone a gas station or convenience store. A lot of the time, there isn't even any cell service!

Thankfully we've never had a breakdown or gotten lost when we've gone through one of these deserted areas, because I'm not too sure what I would do in that situation. With no cell service, who would we have to call on in our time of need?

Isn't it amazing that we have a heavenly Father we can call on at *any* time—no matter what? Our Lord Jesus Christ isn't limited by communication towers, and he's not impacted by even the biggest storms. No matter how lost we are in this life, he is always beside us. That's why prayer is so incredible—because it allows us to talk to him whenever we need to.

Today's passage touches on this—no matter whether we are troubled or joyful, sick or healthy, God earnestly desires to hear our prayers. Furthermore, James writes that the prayers of the righteous (if you've entrusted your life to Jesus, then that's you!) are *powerful* and *effective*. In other words, the Lord hears our prayers and takes them into immediate consideration. He hears our requests and intercedes on our behalf, turning even the crazy parts of our lives into something beautiful.

Now, that doesn't mean that we won't face troubles and trials. We will—every day. Just because the Lord hears all of our prayers doesn't mean he'll answer every one the way we wish he would. (This is actually a good thing—imagine if God granted every little kid's request for unlimited ice cream or 365 days of summer vacation!) The Lord's ways are infinitely higher than our own. So, though he listens to each of our requests, he often answers our prayers in ways vastly different than we imagined.

And that's okay.

Because, as I've said all along, Jesus Christ is our all-powerful, all-knowing tour guide. Even when the route he leads us down seems winding, weird, or even wrong, God knows what he's doing. We can cling tightly to him even amid the bumps in our road of life because he has a plan. When we're feeling lost or frightened about the future, we can turn to the Lord in prayer.

Communication lines are never down between us and our heavenly Father. He'll hear us, and he'll help us. Every time.

Dear Lord Jesus, I'm so grateful for the opportunity to come to you in prayer whenever I need help. I never want to take that for granted. Help me to better see and understand the gift that is my personal relationship with you. Amen.

Every time you pull out your phone today to make a call or send a text, say a short prayer, letting God know what's on your heart. Keeping the communication lines open between us and our Savior is one of the most important things we can do to stay on the right path.

DAY 4: ANTIDOTE TO FEAR

READ PSALM 34

I sought the LORD, and he answered me;
he delivered me from all my fears. – v. 4

DO YOU HAVE any silly travel fears? I, for one, am deathly afraid of escalators. You know—those ever-moving automatic staircases that take passengers between levels of shopping centers, airports, and even department stores? Yes, they're commonplace—and yes, they freak me out.

The thought of clumsy me plus a rotating chain of spiky-toothed stairs is enough to send shivers down my spine. In fact, you'd better hope you never have to ride on an escalator with me, because I would unashamedly cling to your hand while getting on *and* off the Moving Staircase of Doom.

Yes, it's safe to say that I am thoroughly terrified of escalators.

Unfortunately, fear is a very real thing that we all deal with on some level. Getting scared by spiders and snakes (and, yes, escalators) is one thing, but it's no match for the overwhelming anxiety over more serious matters that we will all face at some point in our lives.

But when this happens—when fears and worries and the general stress of life threaten to overwhelm us—we can take heart. Because just like I'll ask whomever I'm with to give me a hand on the escalator, we can ask our Lord and Savior to take away our anxiety and hold us safely and tightly in his completely loving and capable hands.

When the psalmist (in this case, David) wrote this poem, he was a fugitive—a man on the run from the law and hiding in a cave. Yet he sounds happy here, doesn't he? David's words are full of peace and praise as, verse after verse, he sings of the Lord's goodness. God's mercy, glory, and righteousness are all exalted in this prayer of praise. And, again and again, the heart of this psalm rings true: when we lift up our hearts—our hopes and fears and everything else—to the Lord, he not only hears us, but he will answer us. That response might take time—after all, David had to flee not only an angry King Saul but also a wicked Philistine ruler before finding refuge. And that "refuge" was a cold, dark, damp, and dirty cave and a group of vagabonds that could give Robin Hood's merry men a run for their money.

But even when God answers our prayers in ways that seem strange, he *is* answering them. He is working behind the scenes and on our behalf. His plans for us are for good—for a hope and a future. The Lord is not slow in answering our prayers, but his perfect timing reigns supreme. Even when it seems as if our prayers are falling upon deaf ears, they aren't.

God is with us every second of every day, holding our hearts when we're afraid and giving us strength when we need it the most. Our Savior is not intimidated by even our greatest fears, so today let's give them over to him. Let's do as David did and take refuge in the loving arms of Christ. When we fall on him, he will hold us, lift us up, and sustain us as we continue on our journey down the beautiful, perfect path that he has for us.

Dear God, I'm afraid today. Please be with me—come down to hold me. Carry me. Walk with me through this. Help me to feel your presence, both now and forever. Amen.

. . . .

When you feel alone today or overwhelmed by anxiety, simply call upon the name of Jesus. Even if you don't have any words to express how you're feeling, the Lord understands. He hears you, he loves you, and he will help you through whatever it is you're dealing with today. Write his name here in your best handwriting and think about what it means to be loved and protected by such a mighty Savior.

DAY 5: SPIRITUAL DROUGHTS

READ JEREMIAH 17:5-8

Blessed is the one who trusts in the LORD. ~ v. 7

IF YOU'VE EVER been to a tropical island or beach resort, then you know that there is one word that describes these enchanted places better than any other: *lush.*

Everywhere you look, you're surrounded by greenery—by flowers and trees and bushes and *life.* Though known for their warm weather and sunshine, tropical islands also see their fair share of rain, keeping the hills filled with verdant foliage and the yards of locals brimming with vibrant hibiscus, plumeria, and bougainvillea bushes.

That's part of what gives these islands their charm—all of the life that springs up seemingly from out of nowhere. Even abandoned parking lots are littered with flower petals. The air is filled with the aroma of plumeria and jasmine. It is, in a sense, magical.

So as the tropics are alive with vibrant flowers and greenery, we, too, are made alive in Christ. As today's verse says, the Lord Jesus is sustaining us even through our hardest times.

When we are in the midst of a "drought"—a season in life where nothing feels quite right, when we're uninspired, unmotivated, or flat-out uncomfortable—we don't need to fear. Because when we truly trust in the Lord and give our hopes and dreams and worries and fears over to him, he will sustain us.

No matter what.

I know spiritual droughts are tough; I've been through my fair share of them, and I still have a lot more life left to live. We are traveling through a broken, fallen, and sinful world where struggles of every sort are, quite frankly, unavoidable. It's impossible for us to spend our entire lives dodging the drama of everyday life, but here's the good news—*we don't need to.*

When struggles crop up in our lives, we don't have to stew over or fret about them. Sure, we will all deal with huge problems—sometimes more than one at a time—but we're not in this fight alone. The Lord sees us. He is always with us. And he loves us completely.

If you're in the midst of a drought today, take heart. Cling to the words in Jeremiah. Even in our greatest struggles, we can be free of fear because the Lord is holding on to us, placing us exactly where we need to be to grow. To *thrive.*

Dear Lord Jesus, my life feels complicated and messy today, and my spirit is exhausted. Take care of me—plant me by the streams of your living water—and strengthen me to continue my walk down the path you have for me. Amen.

....

Take some time today to get away—whether that's at a park, in a coffee shop, or even in your bedroom—and spend some time with the Lord. Pray, read your Bible, and let him refresh you with his love, mercy, and goodness.

DAY 6: FIRST THINGS FIRST

READ MATTHEW 6:25-43

> *Seek first his kingdom and his righteousness. . . .*
> *Do not worry about tomorrow.* ~ *vv. 33-34*

WHEN YOU GO on a trip, what's the very first thing you like to do when you arrive at your destination?

Do you hit the ground running and spend your first day exploring? Maybe you head straight for a local restaurant to get a taste of the town or immediately check into your hotel and take a nap—jet lag *is* a thing, after all! Or, if you're like me, the first thing you do is unpack your suitcase.

No matter where I'm going or how long I'll be staying there, I love making sure that everything I brought with me is neatly organized and shipshape in my home away from home. And I know that if I don't tackle the unpacking first thing, I'll likely forget to *ever* get my stuff completely organized.

It's important for me to get unpacked and settled in before I truly begin my vacation, and we as Christians must also make an effort to "unpack" our worries before the Lord as we prepare to start each day.

Let's face it—we live in a hurry-hurry, rush-rush, go-go-go kind of society. Even our best intentions of setting aside time to spend with God can be sidetracked by a single notification on our phone. Sometimes the "important" stuff in life (that really *isn't* all that important . . .) gets in the way of what matters most.

When we allow life's little problems—all of those things that *seem* like a big deal but really aren't—to take first place in our hearts and minds, we're opening the door to a whole truckload of unwanted worry and stress. Starting the day with a review of our to-do list might feel productive but, more often than not, it can leave us feeling overwhelmed and overrun with the demands of life. But when we start the day by seeking the Lord, we're giving ourselves an opportunity to quiet our spirits and fill our souls with peace and rest.

No matter what's on our agenda on any given day, I know for a fact that it goes so much better when we bring our hearts to the Lord first. When we spend time in prayer, laying our hopes and dreams and worries and concerns before the throne of the One who loves us the most, we are setting the stage for success before we even begin.

Dear Lord, thank you for the incredible opportunity to come to you in prayer at any time of the day. Help me to become more intentional in seeking you first and resting in your peace every morning. Amen.

. . . .

Make it a point for the next week to start each day with prayer—before you even hop out of bed! Write your prayers in the space below, or pray silently. There's no right or wrong way for us to talk to God as long as we're sharing our hearts with him!

_____

_____

_____

_____

_____

_____

_____

_____

DAY 7: OUR FORTRESS

READ PSALM 94:16-23

> *When anxiety was great within me,*
> *your consolation brought me joy.* ~ *v. 19*

THE CITY OF VALLETTA, MALTA, is incredible. Nicknamed "the Fortress City," it is abounding in bastions and forts, stony walls and ancient citadels. Polished cannons stand at the ready atop a massive fortress, pointed out toward the glistening turquoise harbor. Ancient bell towers stand proudly. Ramparts rise up to meet the sky. And deep within the city lies one of the most stunning monuments to the Christian faith that I have ever seen. The massive, majestic interior of St. John's Co-Cathedral defies even the most flowery human descriptions, so do me a favor and go look it up yourself.

What's really incredible is how safe and secure this teeny tiny island (less than one hundred square miles!) truly feels. Though it's merely a speck in the wide Mediterranean Sea, Malta is a fortress.

And that's exactly what Jesus is for us.

Today's passage tells us that God is our fortress. He is the Rock upon which we stand; the place we run to for refuge. The fortifications of Malta have stood strong for hundreds upon hundreds of years, but our Savior has stood strong since the very beginning of time.

When we're attacked by anxiety, God really is our refuge. The psalmist writes in today's passage that when we cry out to the Lord, he not only hears us but also supports us. When we're failing—when we're falling—Jesus is waiting to catch us. To carry us. To hold us close.

It's not always easy to cry out. Sometimes our fear overwhelms us, convincing us that calling to the Lord for help is hopeless. Pointless. That it would be easier just to give up. But these thoughts are *not* true. They're lies from the devil, who attempts to keep us from the security of the Lord's mighty stronghold. And we can't let the enemy win.

That's why, when we're under attack spiritually, mentally,

or physically, we can't afford to surrender. We have to run—with all the strength and energy and perseverance we have left in our bodies—all the way to Jesus. Because there we can find rest not just in his fortress but in his very arms.

Friends, he hears us. He sees us. He *loves* us. And I can promise you this—no matter how great the anxiety in our souls today, God is greater.

He is *always* greater.

Dear Lord, thank you for being my fortress and giving me a place of rest in your ever-loving arms. It's not always easy for me to admit when I'm afraid, but I know that when I do, you hear me and will rescue me. Help me, Lord, to fall on you the next time I'm overwhelmed. I want to experience your peace and rest. Your protection. Amen.

....

The psalmist didn't have to use any fancy wording when he was struggling. All he needed to say was "My foot is slipping," and the Lord rescued him. The next time you feel overwhelmed, simply cry out to the Lord and let him rescue you. An honest, heartfelt plea for help is just as powerful as any expertly worded prayer.

DAY 8: ROCK OF OUR SALVATION

READ PSALM 61

> *When my heart is overwhelmed; lead me to the rock*
> *that is higher than I. ~ v. 2 (NKJV)*

I MIGHT BE a little biased, being a PNW girl and all, but I think the Oregon coast is one of the most stunning places in the entire world. Something about being surrounded by untamed, crashing waves, windswept coastlines, and towering sea cliffs speaks to my heart in a way that few other things can. But my favorite part of the Oregon coast has to be the sea stacks.

These massive pillars of rock rise high amid the waves, towering over the rest of the beach. Oregon's most famous sea stack, Haystack Rock, stands well over two hundred feet tall. Talk about impressive!

My favorite sea stack, though, isn't this famous natural monolith—it's a smaller, lesser-known formation off the coast of a tiny town named Bandon. It's affectionately known as Face Rock. This massive boulder (which really *does* look like a face!) in the midst of the water has a stirring, almost mournful quality that is only augmented by the local lore surrounding the formation.

Whenever I visit this part of the coast—which, I must admit, is pretty often—I can't help but sit and stare at Face Rock. Especially on blustery days, there's something oddly empowering about watching the waves crash over this massive rock formation. No matter how fierce the wind and the waves, they are never any match for Face Rock. Even on the stormiest days—when sea-foam smashes against the rocks and splashes into the air like a rocket—Face Rock is unmoved. It stands, tall and proud, amid the chaos and the storm.

And that's how we can stand too.

We can stand tall because God is our Rock. He is greater than our fears, and he's greater than the struggles we're facing. He is greater than anything in this world because he *created* this world. He breathed each and every one of us into existence. And even when it's hard to believe, we can know that he will never leave us.

If you're feeling frightened or anxious or just plain worn out today, do as the psalmist said and cry out to the Lord. Find rest in his mercy and goodness. Let him be your Rock—a place of comfort and hope and solace. No matter what you're going through in life, the Lord can give you rest.

Face Rock isn't obliterated by even the most turbulent waves, and, when we put our faith in the One who loves us the most, we won't be washed away by the trials of this world. With him on our side, we have something better than a sea stack to hold us up. We have the Lord God. Our shelter. Our comforter. Our Rock.

Dear God, thank you that no matter what struggles I'm facing in my life, you give me the strength I need to stand firm. Thank you for being the One I can run to when my soul is weary. Thank you for being my Rock. Amen.

How can standing upon Christ's solid foundation help you in the midst of your struggles today?

_____

_____

_____

_____

_____

_____

DAY 9: YOUR WILL BE DONE

READ 1 JOHN 5:13-15

> *If we ask anything according to his will, he hears us. And if we know that he hears us—whatever we ask—we know that we have what we asked of him. - vv. 14-15*

IF YOU'VE EVER taken a cruise or been to a resort or an all-you-can-eat restaurant, chances are you've experienced a pretty incredible buffet. If you haven't, then picture this:

You're standing in a room surrounded by what feels like miles and miles of countertops in front of an endless row of steaming dishes, piles of pastries, and more cookies than your heart could ever desire. What's more, there are chefs and servers bustling around everywhere, working behind grills and preparing made-to-order specialties like omelets or sandwiches. Whatever it is that you have a hankering for, it's practically guaranteed that you can find it at a buffet.

In the same way that you can visit one of these glorious buffets and ask for—and receive—almost any food your heart desires, we are told in the book of 1 John that God hears every single one of our requests. But God isn't a buffet. He isn't a vending machine, either.

Often we are tempted to use today's verse to justify asking God for literally anything. By removing that one little clause—"according to his will"—we're essentially trying to say that the Lord will give us anything we ask for. And that's *wrong*! When we bring our requests before the Lord, there is absolutely no guarantee that he will answer our prayers in the way we're hoping for. But there's an even better promise hidden in today's verses.

God hears us.

He is always listening. Always. Sometimes I picture him listening to our ridiculous requests with a half smile and a knowing laugh, and other times nodding along compassionately. Because when our requests are in *accordance with his will*, the Lord answers our prayers.

When we talk with God, we shouldn't ask, "What's in it for me?" or only consider everything that *we* want to get out of our time spent with him. Instead, let's approach our heavenly Father with humble hearts. We should come to him not just to ask for favors but to ask for his favor upon our lives. The moment we stop treating prayer as a vending machine or "blessing buffet" is the moment we begin living more whole-heartedly for Jesus. By praying not to satisfy our own selfish desires but to more fully follow God's will, we will be one step closer to knowing our Father's heart for us.

And that's a wonderful thing.

Lord, I confess that when I get flustered or anxious, I tend to turn my prayers into an arm-length "wish list" of requests. Help me to focus less on myself and more on you when I spend time with you in prayer. Forgive me for asking for things that only fit my own will, and help me to seek to follow your will through friendship with you. Amen.

....

Remember the phrase "not my will but thy will" during your prayer time this week. How can focusing more on the Father's will help you align your own prayers and desires with his?

_____

_____

_____

_____

_____

_____

_____

DAY 10: PREPARED OR SCARED?

READ JOHN 14:1-4; 25-27

> *Peace I leave with you; my peace I give you.* ~ *v. 27*

ONE TIME WHEN I went on vacation, I got sick. Like, *really* sick. Even though I was in one of my favorite places in the world, I spent two entire days holed up in my room, fighting a fever and begging my mom to run down the road for more NyQuil. It was miserable. Although I ended up pushing through that nasty flu bug and having one of the greatest trips of my life, the realization that I could get *that* sick—while having the time of my life, no less—scared me.

The next time I flew somewhere, I was prepared. I doused myself with hand sanitizer in between every security checkpoint, avoided as many sniffling toddlers as I could manage, and popped vitamin C capsules like they were candy. I wasn't just prepared—I was *scared*.

Sometimes that line between *prepared* and *scared* is so fine that we can't even see it.

Can't stop thinking about which crowd to hang out with, what to spend your allowance on, or whether you've studied enough for an end-of-the-week test? It's possible you're just being prepared—fully educating yourself to prevent any bad decision-making. Which is all well and good.

But when that preparation turns into an obsession . . . that's when we have a problem on our hands. Overthinking and worrying are the best of friends. After all, you can't be *worried* about something if you're not thinking about it.

When we start to overthink—running stats and scenarios over and over in our minds—we're opening the door to worry. And that's dangerous. A calm, rational (and oftentimes necessary!) internal discussion can easily become a panicked mental frenzy of fear. What's worse, once we're stuck in this frenzy, it's nearly impossible to escape.

That's where the Lord's peace comes in.

Jesus Christ himself is speaking straight to us in today's passage. And what does he say? "Do not let your hearts be troubled. . . . My peace I give you. . . . Do not be afraid."

The Lord's peace goes far beyond what we, with our human hearts and minds and feeble understanding, could even begin to comprehend. This peace that the Bible speaks of is the Hebrew *shalom*—a word that encompasses not just our English definition of peace but also something deeper. This peace—this shalom—stands for wholeness. The sort of wholeness that, perhaps, can only be truly found when we unite our own thoughts with those of the Lord's.

And when we align our minds with God's peace, we will discover so much more than the kind of tranquility that is found atop a mountain or alongside a tropical beach. No longer will we need to let overthinking and overanalyzing plague our thoughts and minds. Because when we are one with the Lord in spirit, we discover the shalom that makes us truly whole.

Dear Lord Jesus, thank you for your shalom—the peace that you have given to each one of us. Help me to feel your presence when

I'm overwhelmed by my thoughts and worries, and let me fully understand the kind of peace that comes from being united with you in Christ. Amen.

....

Use the following pages to journal about a time when your soul felt completely, totally at rest. How can you unite yourself with the Lord on a daily basis so that you might more often feel this kind of peace in your life?

bonus adventure: road trip!

Ready for an adventure? Grab your backpack and a pair of hiking boots (or at least walking shoes) because this date with God is all about getting out and exploring his creation!

Have you ever played tourist in your own hometown? If not, there's no better time to start than right now. So whip up a batch of my favorite Italian lemon cookies, stash them in your bag, and set off on a walk with the Lord.

Italian Lemon Cookies

1 ¼ CUPS FLOUR

¼ CUP + 2 TABLESPOONS CORNSTARCH

2 ½ TABLESPOONS LEMON JUICE

½ TABLESPOON LEMON ZEST (+ extra for topping cookies)

¼ TEASPOON SALT

¾ CUP + 2 TABLESPOONS SOFTENED BUTTER

½ CUP POWDERED SUGAR

LEMON GLAZE (recipe to follow)

1. Whisk together flour, cornstarch, lemon zest, and salt. In a separate bowl, beat butter and powdered sugar until fluffy. Add half of the flour mixture and lemon juice, beating to combine. Combine remaining flour mixture, stirring to form

a slightly sticky dough. If the dough seems extra sticky, add another tablespoon or two of flour.

2. Transfer the dough to a piece of parchment paper and roll into a log that is about 1½ inches wide. Refrigerate for an hour before unwrapping and cutting the dough into ½-inch slices. Place on a parchment-lined cookie sheet and refrigerate for 20 minutes.

3. Bake at 320° F for five minutes, then raise the temperature to 350° and bake for about nine more minutes or until lightly golden. Let cool completely, then top with lemon glaze and sprinkle with remaining lemon zest.

Lemon Glaze

JUICE OF ONE LEMON (+ more for desired consistency)

1 TABLESPOON LEMON ZEST

1½ CUPS POWDERED SUGAR

Combine all ingredients in a small bowl to taste, adding additional lemon juice if glaze is too thick.

Now that your cookies are ready, it's time to plan your adventure. What natural wonders exist right outside your door? Set aside a day to take a hike or spend time at your favorite city park. Maybe you have an old tree house from when you were little—bring up a cozy blanket and pillow and have a campout in your own backyard. If you'd like your adventure to take on more of an urban feel, spend the day downtown or hang out at a cute coffee shop or library reading room. Maybe you've always wanted to explore a nearby city or small town. Find a friend or family member willing to tag along, and turn your time with the Lord into a mini Bible study. Once you've decided on and arrived at your dream destination, put on some music (I've included a few of my favorite worship songs below) and dive into these journaling questions:

JOURNALING QUESTIONS

- What "speed bumps" have I been hitting lately? How have they affected my journey?

- How could I use these apparent roadblocks to grow closer to the Lord?

- What dreams has the Lord been laying on my heart recently?

- If I could make one of these dreams come true, which one would it be? What is fueling my desire to do that thing?

- How could God use this dream for his glory?

- What small steps could I take to make this dream come true?

SUGGESTED SOUNDTRACK

- "You Already Know" BY JJ HELLER

- "Great Is Thy Faithfulness (Beginning to End)"
  BY ONE SONIC SOCIETY

- "Just as I Am" BY TRAVIS COTTRELL

- "Blessed Assurance (My King Is Coming)"
  BY MATTHEW WEST

- "Graves into Gardens" BY ELEVATION WORSHIP

- "Come to Jesus (Untitled Hymn)"
  BY JASON LOVINS BAND

- "Watch Over Me" BY AARON SHUST

- "Into the Sea (It's Gonna Be Okay)" BY TASHA LAYTON

- "Always Good" BY ANDREW PETERSON

PS—I know from experience that this soundtrack makes great walking music. Strap on those hiking boots and let the worship music wash over you as you ponder how you can start living out the dreams that God has given you *right now*.

CHAPTER 6

The Layover

DAY 1: BETWEEN FLIGHTS

READ JOSHUA 1:1-9

> *The LORD your God will be with you wherever you go.* – v. 9

HAVE YOU EVER had a layover? It's when you're stuck waiting between connecting flights at an airport—and sometimes you have to wait a *long* time. Usually during a layover I end up eating overpriced junk food, sleeping in uncomfortable chairs, and walking aimlessly around the airport as I count the minutes until my next flight's boarding call. In short, a layover can be pretty miserable.

What, then, happens when we experience a layover in our own life—when it feels like we're in between flights and our heavenly Pilot has disappeared?

As much as I wish the Christian life could be filled with one mountaintop experience after the other, it's impossible for us to experience that sort of spiritual high all the time. Sometimes we feel distant from the Lord for no particular reason. We're going through a layover. A dry spell. During these times, it can be hard for us to sense the Lord's presence. We might question whether or not he's even there.

It's times like these when I can't help but feel incredibly grateful for reminders like the one in this chapter's key verse—that God is *always* with us.

In today's reading, we meet Joshua during a pretty crazy time in his life—he's been ordered to take the place of Moses and is preparing to lead the Lord's people into the Promised Land. I don't know about you, but if I'd been Joshua, I would've been terrified. Maybe that's why God told Joshua not once or twice but *three times* to "be strong and courageous." Even more encouraging than that, though, are those last three words that the Lord says: "wherever you go."

With these words, God is making his plans clear. No matter what Joshua does and where his journey takes him, he can rest in the assurance that his heavenly Father is right there with him, guiding and protecting him through every part of his journey.

So, too, does God have his holy hand over us. Even when we feel alone . . . we're not. God has a plan for us that's far greater than anything we could possibly imagine, and he's walking alongside us, working all things for *good* in our lives. Joshua was about to fight giants and conquer nations. It wasn't an easy task, and I can only imagine how alone and intimidated he must have been feeling in that moment.

But with the Lord God on his side, the young, inexperienced Israelite managed to do amazing things. What's more, just as the Holy Spirit never left nor forsook Joshua, he will never forsake us either. Whether we've been going through a spiritual dry spell—stuck waiting on God during the longest layover of our life—or we've been feeling the Lord's presence every second of every day, Jesus Christ remains the same.

He's right here. With us. Always.

As we explore this chapter further, let's be encouraged by this reminder. The Lord has called us to do amazing things, but he hasn't sent us out on a solo expedition. He isn't going to abandon ship. No! Instead, our God is watching out for us. His holy hand is on all that we do.

And with his help, we are going to go far.

Dear God, what a comfort it is to know that, even though I can't see you or touch you or audibly hear your voice, you are always with me. That can be so hard for me to remember, Lord, especially when life is hard and I feel like I'm left waiting on you. Help me to feel more of your presence today, even if I'm in a waiting season of life. Amen.

....

Write down this chapter's key verse so you can memorize it, then take some time to think through these questions:

Do you feel like you're in the middle of a layover? What are you waiting on in your life? How can you put your trust in the Lord and his presence during this season?

_____

_____

_____

_____

_____

_____

DAY 2: WHILE WE WAIT

READ ZEPHANIAH 3:8-17

> *The LORD your God is with you,*
> *the Mighty Warrior who saves. ~ v. 17*

WHEN I WAS LITTLE, I always stashed a cherished doll or stuffed animal in my suitcase before I left on a trip. Whether it was an overnight at my grandma's or a twelve-hour drive to Disneyland, I wanted to ensure that one of my "snuggle buddies" would be with me every step of the way. I remember resting comfortably during my first airplane ride and smiling at the idea that one of my beloved stuffed animals (a raggedy panda creatively named Pandy) was tucked safely away in my suitcase in the cargo hold beneath my feet.

When we're in the midst of a waiting season in our own life, it's easy to get stressed out. Unsettled. Maybe even a little panicky. Depending on what we're waiting for and how long we've *been* waiting, it can grow harder and harder for us to be patient. What do we do while we wait? Has God really forgotten about us? Is he too busy helping everybody else?

The ancient Israelites were waiting too. In today's passage, we read a message from a gracious heavenly Father to his people. Israel had done terrible things, continually rejecting God's sovereignty and trying time and time again to forge their own path. God judged them for this, but he also promised to renew them and save them.

But there's a catch. One that goes like this: "'Therefore wait for me,' declares the LORD" (verse 8). Israel's salvation wouldn't come overnight. The answers to our problems, the miracle we've been asking for, and the rains to quench our dry spell won't come overnight either. Instead, they come slowly. After days, weeks, or even *years* of prayer.

During waiting times like these, it's easy to feel stuck. But in the same way the Israelites received instruction to wait on the Lord and trust in his name, we, too, must have patience in the waiting. When we close our eyes, take a deep breath, and trust that God is near, an ever-present help in our trouble, we are not only exercising our faith but also filling our hearts with the Lord's everlasting peace.

Just like knowing that my favorite stuffed animal was safely nestled in the luggage hold beneath my seven-year-old feet was a huge help during my first airplane flight, knowing that the Lord is near to bring us comfort even through our waiting seasons is the greatest solace imaginable.

Dear God, sometimes waiting feels hard—it can even be scary. Thank you for standing by me and comforting me. Help me to experience more of your presence in this time, Lord. In Jesus' name I pray, amen.

What little pieces of God's goodness get you through the days when it's harder to "see" him? How can you seek out and cling to these reminders in your times of waiting?

DAY 3: OUR PLANS VS. HIS

READ ISAIAH 40:27-31

> *The LORD is the everlasting God. . . .*
> *His understanding no one can fathom. ~ v. 28*

I AM THE WORLD'S WORST TRAVEL AGENT.

Like, ever.

I'll never forget the time I booked a weekend adventure for my mom and me in a cottage at what was billed as a "luxury waterfront glamping resort." If I'd considered it fun to wave a broom at the ceiling because said cottage was actually a miniature bread box with a smoke detector that couldn't tell shower steam from a raging inferno, to spend the weekend headachy and hangry because this "resort" was stuck in the middle of nowhere and I hadn't thought to bring food, or to communicate with front-desk people who were cranky the whole time, then this weekend would've been the highlight of my year.

As it was, I spent most of my time wondering whether to laugh or cry. (Spoiler alert: I laughed. A lot.) My confidence in my vacation-planning abilities only shrank when, not long after that, we stayed at a different hotel in the same area and had one of the best weekends *ever*. Guess who made all the plans that time? (Hint: it wasn't me.) I could hardly believe I was visiting the same place!

My mom's plans were better than anything I could've imagined, and, in the same way, the path God has laid out for us is way more incredible than even our wildest dreams. He's plotting the course of our life step-by-step.

But sometimes that's scary—especially when we're in an unexpected time of waiting or when we feel like the Lord has gone silent.

Let's face it—God's ways are not our own. They never will be. His timing and his plans are often vastly different from ours. Sometimes that makes life complicated. But that's not a bad thing. If we would trust an experienced travel agent and give them free rein to make the best decisions for us regarding a trip to a faraway destination, then we must also surrender our own hopes and dreams to the Lord.

God is infinitely more powerful than our fears or present circumstances. In our waiting seasons, it's easy to think that he has abandoned us. That's certainly how the Israelites felt when Isaiah prophesied to them in today's featured passage. They were waiting for a Deliverer—a Messiah—but he wasn't coming on their time. They felt as if their pleas were falling on deaf ears. As if God had turned his back on them. But he hadn't. He didn't. He never will.

We all have hopes and dreams and an itinerary for our life that we'd love to see come to pass. When the things we're hoping for don't happen on our time or our plans change altogether, it can be hard to see how the Lord is at work. But God's understanding goes far deeper than our own. He knows what he's doing, and he hasn't abandoned us. We can trust him in the waiting because we know that his plans for us are nothing but *good*.

Dear God, my plans and hopes and dreams are so very precious to me, but your Word tells me that your understanding is much deeper than mine. Help me to have faith in the beautiful mystery of your ways and put my trust in you as you work in my life. In Jesus' name, amen.

....

Write down some of your hopes and dreams in the column on the left. Then consider what God's path for you might look like. What has he been showing you lately? On the right, list some of the ways that he might be calling you to serve him. Then compare the two.

DAY 4: THE REAL CHRISTMAS LIGHT

READ PSALM 18:28-36

My God turns my darkness into light. ~ v. 28

ONE YEAR during the holiday season, I got the opportunity to spend an evening in the city and take a limo ride to look at Christmas lights. Now, I've always thought that *my* family got into the holiday spirit, but I was completely unprepared for what I saw during that drive. The house that stood out to me the most featured a life-size sleigh (complete with reindeer!) "flying" through the sky. I'm sure it was cleverly suspended from the majestic oak trees flanking the front yard, but any supports were invisible in the dark of night, making the effect nothing short of magical.

That entire neighborhood was lit up from top to bottom, twinkling with fairy lights and gleaming even on one of the coldest, rainiest days of the year. The cheer and joy and over-all wonder of the Christmas season turned a dreary day into something truly special.

Today's passage praises the Lord for doing much the same thing. Our featured verse says that God turns our darkness into light, and it's true! The heavenly One who is the source of the world's Christmas magic and the Creator of all earthly beauty is the same One who is guiding each of our lives.

Not only does Jesus bring light to our lives, but he also gives us the strength to do his will. The psalmist writes that the

Lord is making us strong and training us for battle—because there *will* be battles. Every day that we wake up, get out of bed, and make a choice to live for Christ's Kingdom, we're going to face opposition. There are people in this world who would love to convince us that our beliefs are wrong. That we're foolish for trusting in a God we can't hear or see. And there's a very real, very cruel devil who wants nothing more than to make our lives miserable.

Sometimes when we fight battles against the enemy, we can tell that the Lord is right there with us. We can feel him in our hearts so deeply that, when we turn around, it's nearly a shock to see that he isn't standing right there. Other times we feel that we've been left to complete the journey on our own—even if we don't know the way. We might be asked to make a difficult decision that no amount of soul-searching, Bible reading, or prayer seems to answer.

But there is *always* an answer, and there is *always* a way. Jesus Christ paved the road to eternal life through his death and resurrection, and that road is all we need. It leads through every moment of your life, every choice you have ever made and every difficult decision that is yet to come. And though, as we learned a few chapters ago, the gate that leads to eternal life is narrow, the psalmist writes that the path God has laid out for us is broad so we don't stumble and fall (verse 36).

The Lord knows us, and he knows our hearts. Even when we can't feel him at work in our lives, he is there—behind the scenes. A light in the darkness. Ready to give us strength when we need it the most.

Dear God, thank you for never leaving my side. Thank you for lighting the way when my path seems dark. Please give me more of your strength today, and help me to live for you in everything. Amen.

....

What shadowy spot in your life could use a bit of Christ's light today? Write out a prayer here, asking him for help in that specific area.

_____

_____

_____

_____

_____

_____

_____

_____

_____

_____

_____

DAY 5: SECRET BEACHES

READ JEREMIAH 23:23-24

> *"Who can hide in secret places so that I cannot see them?"*
> *declares the LORD. ~ v. 24*

HAVE YOU EVER been to a secret beach? These marvelous stretches of sand are often referred to as "hidden gems" by guidebooks and touted as "best-kept secrets" by travel blogs, and they are truly magical. Even though most so-called secret beaches get enough publicity these days that they aren't as private as they once were, there's still something a little thrilling about stepping onto a near-deserted stretch of sand in the wee hours of the morning.

My favorite semisecret beach is Baby Beach in Lahaina, Hawaii. Not only is there a dazzling stretch of sand but there's also a sparkling, calm bay with an incredible snorkeling reef just offshore. In the quiet morning hours, when this secluded beach is at its most peaceful, there's a good chance you'll be able to swim among tropical fish *and* sea turtles! It's no secret that this enchanted white-sand crescent is nothing less than paradise.

Even if we were to locate the most secret, remote beach in the world, we wouldn't be able to hide from the Lord. In today's key verse, God tells us that no one can hide from him. Whether we travel to the ends of the earth or tuck ourselves into a tiny ball in the farthest corner of our messy closet, God still sees us. How much more, then, must he be watching out for us when we are living in perfect communion with him?

We cannot hide from the Lord, and God will not hide himself from us. Yes, it's true that there will be times in our lives when he feels far away, but he is never gone. The Lord is with us in all that we do. He's a constant source of power and protection even when we're going through massive amounts of turbulence in our lives.

There is never a moment that the Lord doesn't see us—that he can't hear our cry. We could climb to the top of the highest mountain or fall into the deepest pit and the Holy Spirit would follow us. That's just who he is. He is a Father intimately acquainted with each of his children—a holy God who loves each of us as his very own.

Being a daughter of the King isn't just a pretty platitude or something we say for fun. For the rest of our lives and on into eternity, we will have the greatest honor of being seen and known and loved by our incredible Creator.

Even when we feel unreachable—as though we're in a place where God couldn't possibly forgive us or save us—the Lord is at hand. He is omniscient and omnipresent. He's everywhere all at once. He fills heaven and earth, and he sees and loves *you*. No matter what you're facing today, it's never too much for God to handle.

Dear Lord Jesus, thank you for never leaving me. It's such a comfort to know that, wherever I run, you will always be with me. Please help me feel more of your presence today, I pray. Amen.

Have you ever tried to hide from the Lord? If so, did today's passage help you understand that time of "hiding" differently?

_____

_____

_____

_____

_____

_____

DAY 6: TRUST THE CAPTAIN

READ PSALM 91

> *He will command his angels concerning you*
> *to guard you in all your ways. ~ v. 11*

SAILING AWAY from port on a cruise ship for the first time is a little overwhelming. Usually you're crowded on the top deck with hundreds of fellow passengers. There's loud music playing, people dancing, flags waving, and the ship's horn blowing. But underneath all of this boisterous sail-away excitement, some people experience something else. Fear.

After all, you're headed out into the open ocean on a ship

that, while it seems massive in port, is ridiculously tiny compared to the great, wide sea. And who's driving (sailing?) this thing anyway? They keep talking about the captain of the ship, but you haven't seen him. For heaven's sake, you haven't even seen the ship's wheel!

In fact, it's a rare occurrence (unless you're a VIP) that you will ever see the captain of the ship during your entire journey. It might feel as if the ship is sailing itself—and, especially during rough waters, that can be a little disconcerting.

During my last cruise, though, I found a surprise on one of the decks: a peek-a-boo bridge! The bridge is the place where the ship's officers perform their navigational duties, and getting to peer down into this special area of the ship and watch as the crew charted a perfect course through the stormy waters ahead was a special treat. It was such a sweet reminder that, even though I couldn't usually see anyone steering the ship, the captain was always there. Watching out for me—and for all the other passengers, too.

Just like the captain and crew of that ship were there, making sure the ship stayed on course even when I couldn't see them working, so too is the Lord continually at work in and through our lives. There are times when we can't see or feel him steering us in the right direction, but that doesn't mean he has deserted us.

All good things take time, and discovering God's ultimate plan and purpose for our lives is one of the best things that can ever happen to us. So we must be patient—joyful in hope and calm through the waiting—as God guides us.

These times of waiting are what build our perseverance

and help us grow as believers, but they also serve to make the times when we *can* see God at work even more rewarding. It was such a treat to finally get a peek at the action on the ship's bridge during my last cruise, but it's an even more incredible thrill when we get to watch God work in our lives. So, today, let's cling fast to the promises found in Psalm 91. God is with us, guarding us in all of our ways. Even when we're sailing through uncharted waters, we have a great and mighty Captain who is leading and guiding us. With him working on our behalf, we have nothing to fear.

Dear Lord, thank you for the times when I get to see you at work in my life. Please give me strength and confidence when I can't see you as much. Amen.

....

List some times you have seen God at work in your life and others where he felt far away. How did you stay close to him even through those more difficult times?

_____

_____

_____

_____

_____

_____

_____

_____

_____

_____

DAY 7: YET I WILL REJOICE

READ HABAKKUK 3:17-19

> Yet I will rejoice in the LORD,
> I will be joyful in God my Savior. ~ v. 18

HAVE YOU EVER spent time in a desert?

It's a place with myriad unpleasant paradoxes—blazing hot during the day, freezing cold at night. It's dry and arid and lifeless yet somehow thick with snakes and creepy-crawlies, devoid of most vegetation but filled with prickly cacti. No matter which way I look at it, visiting a desert just for the sake of the *desert* isn't on my bucket list. In fact, deserts are pretty high on my list of places to avoid.

The barren place described in today's passage sounds a bit like a desert itself. Habakkuk writes that the fields yield no crops; the stables are empty. In short, it's a wasteland.

The book of Habakkuk was written during a time when God's people could have easily questioned his plan. In fact, they did—over and over again. Why had their beloved Promised

Land been taken away from them? Why was God allowing the enemy to invade? Why was their God—their heavenly Father who supposedly loved them—not stepping in to save them?

While we may not have experienced an enemy invasion like the one described in Habakkuk, we have probably asked God several of these same questions. We all go through times of trouble in our lives when we question the Lord and his plans for us.

Yet it is often in these times of hopelessness and near-abandonment that we end up seeking God the most. Habakkuk questions the Lord and spends time with him before ending his writings with a prayer of peace and victory, but he also praises him despite his difficult circumstances. So too must we come before the Father with not only our problems but also our praise. It can be difficult to find joy in pain or suffering, but it *is* possible. When we choose to turn our eyes from our burdens to our blessings even in our trials, we will find that the peace that passes all understanding is just a little bit easier to grasp.

In times of trouble, our fears and doubts and questions are often amplified until we can't hear the voice of the Lord even when we try. That's where praise comes in. That's why we need to step back. That's why we need to choose joy—to fix our eyes on Jesus Christ and cry out to him in praise even from the wasteland of our circumstances.

Because he always answers.

That answer might come in a still, small voice—not in the roar of a waterfall or the crash of thunder—but it will be there. Because, as we read today, the Lord—our precious Father—is our strength. He is the one preparing us for all the battles we face in this life. He is walking with us through the wasteland. He is making a way in the wilderness and streams in the desert. He has not left us. He is here with us.

Right now.

Today.

Forever.

And that alone is worthy of our praise.

Dear God, even when this life feels like a wilderness or a desert, I'm so grateful for the comfort of your presence and the gift of your salvation. Thank you that because of you, I can rejoice even during the worst trials. Please give me peace and patience and power in my struggles here on earth, I pray. In your name, amen.

What can you rejoice in today? How has the Lord been blessing you lately so that you can find your joy in him no matter the circumstances?

DAY 8: REFUGE IN THE STORM

READ PSALM 46

> *God is our refuge and strength,*
> *a very present help in trouble. ~ v. 1 (NKJV)*

HAVE YOU EVER needed to take refuge somewhere? When a cruise ship dropped my mom and me off in Spain for the day, we took a bus to see the exterior of the famous Casa Batlló, an incredibly ornate facade designed by the famous art nouveau architect Antoni Gaudí. The front of the house was stunning— a gorgeous mosaic of glass and ceramic—and I took more than my fair share of pictures . . . until it started to rain.

With no sign of the next bus coming anytime soon, I ducked into a covered courtyard, wandered around, and somehow found myself in one of the most incredible cafés I'd ever seen. Not only were there glass cases crowded with baked goods and tiny baguette sandwiches, but there was also a special drink on the menu—hot chocolate. This wasn't your grandma's instant cocoa either. This was literally hot melted chocolate, served in a tiny pink cup and topped with a mountain of rich whipped cream. (It was served with bread to dip in it, which was at once *very weird* and *very good*.)

I definitely found a refuge that day—a place to sit back and enjoy a tiny slice of Spanish life while I waited for the storm to pass. Today's psalm talks about a different kind of refuge—the kind that comes only through trust in God. The refuge that will always be available to us. The refuge that we have tucked deep in our souls. It's a very present help—or, as it can also be translated, "an abundantly available help"—in times of need.

It's not uncommon for any of us to be in need during this life. Whether we face relationship difficulties, health problems, long periods of waiting for a prayer to be answered, or any other kind of trial, the Lord is always there. Even when his will seems hard to understand, *he has not left us.* God remains a shelter for us during every moment of every day. We might feel frustrated sometimes and wonder why the Lord isn't making all of his ways clear, but that doesn't need to be our main focus. What matters most is having confidence in our all-knowing, all-seeing Father, who's watching out for us.

Regardless of the troubles we encounter over the course of each day, we can take heart in the promises God has given us—that he is our refuge.

This refuge might not be of the baguette-baking, hot chocolate–making kind, but it's even better. God's refuge is a place of peace and not fear, of love and not hate, of strength and not weakness. Whatever battles we are fighting today, let us find refuge in the arms of the One who loves us the most.

Lord, even though I don't know or understand what you're doing in my life today, I'm thankful for the opportunity to take refuge in you. Please hold me close and give me strength as I prepare to set out on the next step of my journey. Amen.

Take a minute today to simply be alone with God. Let him be your refuge. Pray to him or simply sit and be still. Rest in his presence and feel his peace. (And, if you have the opportunity, make yourself a cup of hot chocolate while you're at it!)

DAY 9: SEARCHING FOR SIGNS

READ JOSHUA 24:14-18

> *He . . . did those great signs in our sight,*
> *and preserved us in all the way that we went.* ~ *v. 17 (NKJV)*

I'VE ALWAYS KNOWN better than to ask for a sign.

But once, on a prayer retreat to the Oregon Coast during which I would make one of the biggest decisions of my entire life, I slipped. I'd been straining for days to hear God's voice, yet he seemed strangely silent. I sensed his presence as I prayed, yes, but I felt as if he had left me to make the decision on my own.

So I did it—I put out a fleece.

If you're wondering why on earth I would put out a fleece and where in the world I found a willing sheep at the coast—don't worry, I'm not being literal. Check out Gideon and his story in Judges chapter 6. Long story short, he was a little nervous about what God had planned for him, so he went through a series of silly "tests" in which he asked God to more clearly reveal his will. Not exactly the smartest move.

Anyway, as I strolled along the sandy seashore, kicking aside broken sand dollars and water-tumbled pebbles, I let the words slip out: "I'd know exactly what God wanted me to do if he gave me a sand dollar. A whole one."

By the end of that trip, I was heading home with a perfectly whole sand dollar and one very made-up mind. That sand dollar now sits on my dresser, a constant reminder of God's faithfulness and provision.

But you know the funny thing? I didn't find that perfect sand dollar on the shore until several days after I asked for it. During the time between my request and God's answer, I spent a lot of time fasting and praying. And, even before I'd found the sand dollar, I had a feeling I knew what to do. The sand dollar, then, was merely confirmation.

Now, I'm not telling you to drop everything and head to the beach the moment you have a tough decision to make, and I'm certainly not suggesting that you refuse to do anything until you receive a visible sign from the Lord. What I'm encouraging you to do, friends, is *wait*.

Don't try to make God answer before his time. Seek peace and pursue that as you pray over your problems. Get advice from those closest to you. Use the gifts God has given you— the people he has put in your life, the passions he has given you with which to worship him, and the precious gift of his Word—to help you make big decisions . . . and then wait some more.

Because the Lord always speaks. Sometimes it's through a sign like the one he gave me, but, more often, it is simply through his presence and his Word. Whether he gives us a sign or not, God is preserving us in all the ways we go. He is walking in step with us, ready to be our Helper in the midst of the troubles we face.

So be alert. Watch and wait for the Lord. Be ready for him to speak.

When we are quiet, we *will* find his peace.

Dear God, I need your wisdom and guidance today. Speak to me, Lord, and strengthen me as I walk down this difficult path. Give me what I need to make the right decisions, and give me peace in this time of my life, I pray. Amen.

....

How could the Lord be speaking to you and using your everyday encounters with others to make clear his will for your life?

_____

_____

_____

_____

_____

_____

_____

DAY 10: YOU ARE MINE

READ ISAIAH 43:1-7

> *When you pass through the waters,*
> *I will be with you.* ~ v. 2 (NKJV)

I'M NOT the world's best swimmer.

My dog paddle is better than my breaststroke *or* my butterfly. And my backstroke? Forget it!

Even so, that never stops me from jumping wholeheartedly into the waves at the beach. There's something about getting crashed over and thrown about by the turbulent waters that thrills me to no end. In fact, I've been known to go out swimming even during a high-surf advisory. (Yes, I can be a bit of a daredevil . . .)

One time, though, I almost didn't make it back to shore.

The red flags were out that day, but I ignored them as I ran straight into the water with my mom (who is also a daredevil). We splashed and thrashed in the waves, letting the water pick us up and carry us wherever it chose. After all, if the local kids were out swimming, we could handle it too.

And we did for a while—until a sneaker wave cropped up and threw us to the hard sand like we were nothing more than limp rag dolls. The undertow grabbed for us, nearly sucking us straight out to sea, and it was a mad scramble back to dry land. Another wave finally slammed us into the shore with all the force of a wrecking ball.

We were drenched, sand-covered, and exhausted, but we were safe.

God was looking out for my mom and me as we foolishly frolicked in the water on that turbulent day, and he hasn't stopped. He's keeping close watch over *all* of us. Whether we've let our adventurous side get us into trouble or we're working through something hard at school or home, God is walking with us.

Today's featured passage includes this simple reassurance from the Lord: "You are mine" (verse 1).

No matter what mess we manage to get ourselves into, God isn't going to make us fight alone. Through flood or fire, he is there.

While it can be difficult to see his presence when we're in the middle of these storms, we can rest in the promises of his Word. Our Captain has not abandoned ship. Our heavenly Father is still walking with us. Guiding us. Protecting us.

Jesus Christ came to earth and gave his own *life* so we could have a relationship with the Father. If we are worth that great a price, how much must our Lord and Savior care for us?

We are precious creations in Christ, and the Lord has prepared blessings for us. Even in our struggles, he is working everything for our good.

No matter what we are walking through—whether lightning and rain or a field of sunshine and buttercups—let's keep our eyes firmly fixed on the One who loves us enough to call us his own.

Let's find our hope and joy in Jesus Christ.

*Lord, sometimes it feels like I'm about to drown in my problems.
Life in this world isn't always easy. Please sustain me as I walk
through this difficult time. Help me to see you in everything, and
give me strength. In Jesus' name, amen.*

....

God is always with us—wherever we go. How does the
knowledge of that help you find peace amid your struggles?

_____

_____

_____

_____

_____

_____

_____

_____

_____

_____

_____

_____

bonus adventure: finding a station

When you're in a new place, it can be a real chore trying to find a good radio station to listen to in place of your old standby! It can be even more difficult when we try to "tune in" to the Lord through prayer and feel like we're hearing nothing more than static. When our heavenly Guide seems silent, sometimes we need a little extra help from our traveling companions. This next adventure is designed for you and your friends to spend some time together engaging in fellowship as believers. By developing godly relationships, we are creating a tribe of traveling companions who will encourage and inspire us in times when the Lord seems far away.

Even during life's longest layovers, there is always joy to be found—so pull together everything you need for a Greek-inspired hummus tray (ideas below!) and host a girls' night—or day!

Greek Hummus Feast

1 CAN GARBANZO BEANS

1 LARGE GARLIC CLOVE

¼ CUP TAHINI

2½ TABLESPOONS LEMON JUICE

COLD WATER

SALT AND PEPPER TO TASTE

CHOPPED FRESH OREGANO, PINE NUTS OR PISTACHIOS, AND OLIVE OIL (FOR TOPPING)

1. Pulse garbanzo beans, garlic, tahini, and lemon juice in a food processor until smooth. Add water as needed until you reach the desired consistency. (Some people like to keep it semichunky; others love it smooth!) Add salt and pepper to taste.

2. Spread hummus on a tray and top with oregano, nuts, and a drizzle of olive oil. Load the rest of the tray with any or all of the following goodies:

CUCUMBER SLICES

BABY CARROTS

HALVED CHERRY TOMATOES

KALAMATA OLIVES

CRUMBLED FETA CHEESE

PEPPERONCINI

PICKLED RED ONION

PISTACHIOS

FLATBREAD OR PITA CHIPS

IDEAS FOR FUN AND FELLOWSHIP

- Movie Night: Pick a movie based on an inspiring true story, grab a stack of cozy blankets, and snuggle up in your PJs . . . just remember to provide plenty of tissues if the film is supposed to be a tearjerker!

- Spa Day: We all know that a beautiful heart is more important than our physical appearance, but that doesn't mean we can't have fun getting glamorous! Give each other mani-pedis and facials, and experiment with new hairstyles. Don't forget to take a group picture!

- Hike + Picnic: Take your Greek feast on the go and drive to a nearby park or hiking trail. Marvel in God's creation and enjoy the fresh air together.

- Pool Afternoon: If you have access to a pool and it's warm where you live, put on an upbeat playlist, lay the snacks out in the shade, and spend the afternoon splashing in the sunshine!

CHAPTER 7

A Bicycle Built for Two (Or More!)

DAY 1: GOING SOLO? THANKS, BUT NO!

READ DEUTERONOMY 31:1-8

> *He will never leave you nor forsake you.* ~ v. 6

WHAT'S THE FARTHEST you've been from home—by yourself? Have you spent a week at your grandparents' house, gone to summer camp miles away, or participated in a mission trip with your church? I'll admit—despite my love of travel, I'm a bit of a homebody and a *lot* of a family girl. The idea of going off on an adventure alone is . . . not my favorite. When I travel—even to a park across town—it's almost always with family or friends.

How comforting it is, then, to know that God is with us every step of the way in each of our lives. Even when we're by ourselves, he surrounds us with his love and holy presence. He never left nor forsook the Israelites, and he'll never leave us either.

God is our heavenly tour guide—the One who knows all. *He* is the one guiding our steps, directing our path, and bringing us comfort in times of need. God wants to be intimately acquainted with even your innermost thoughts—and he is! No matter what, we can't escape from his presence. And that is a glorious reality indeed.

As we walk through this next chapter together, we're going to be learning more about the wonderful, intimate relationship that God has with each of his people, along with how we can mirror Christ's love for us in our interactions with others across the globe. I hope you're ready for a new adventure, because one is starting . . . right now!

Lord, I know that you're here—right by my side. Your promises in the Bible stand true even today. Give me eyes to see and a heart to listen when you speak words of wisdom into my life. Thank you for your presence, Lord. Today and every day.

....

Do you prefer to travel by yourself or with friends and family? How do you feel when you picture God as your "heavenly tour guide"? And yes, you guessed it—write this chapter's key verse on a piece of paper and stick it somewhere you'll be reminded to repeat it to yourself throughout the day.

_____

_____

_____

_____

_____

_____

DAY 2: NIGHT SHADOWS

READ JAMES 1:16-18

[God] does not change like shifting shadows. ~ v. 17

FOR MY FIFTEENTH BIRTHDAY, my dad got tickets for my mom and me to take a train ride all the way to Seattle (a six-hour trip!). It was a wonderful gift, and this country girl was thrilled over the chance to explore a big city. But one night during the trip, my mom and I got lost. Without a phone. We'd attended a concert near the Space Needle and were convinced that, since we could see the Space Needle from our hotel, we'd be able to walk back without difficulty.

We were wrong.

When we stepped out of the concert hall, the night shadows had grown long and suddenly nothing was as it seemed.

Thank goodness that we don't have to spend our lives like that—wandering around without direction or purpose. Instead, we are children of the God of all the earth, the One who has good gifts in store for his kids. He doesn't shift and change like the shadows in those alleyways. His plans are never altered.

Instead, our God is bold. Strong. In control. His ways are good, and his love for us is overwhelming. This God is our tour guide—the One who has the ultimate say over our itinerary.

On that dark night in the middle of the big city, my mom and I put our heads together and combed the streets until we found a twenty-four-hour supermarket where one of the clerks took pity on us and called for a cab. If not for their kindness and compassion, we'd still be wandering aimlessly up and down Seattle alleys to this day!

Just as our Lord is an ever-present help in times of trouble, we too can be a soft spot—a place of peace and rest and reassurance—for those around us to land when they need help. God's incredible, boundless love lives within us, filling us to overflowing so we can extend his goodness to others through our thoughts, words, and actions.

We can bless others richly by showing them this kind of love and faithfulness, whether that's by offering a friend a shoulder to cry on during a difficult time, delivering a warm meal to a family in need, or calling a cab for two lost and tired tourists.

Dear God, I'm so grateful to have you on my side. Help me learn to trust and honor you as I walk down the path you have for me. Thank you for your unchanging love, and help me share it with the people in my life who are hurting. Amen.

What examples of God's faithfulness have you experienced in your life? How can you show others this same sort of dependability?

_____

_____

_____

_____

_____

_____

_____

_____

_____

_____

_____

DAY 3: STANDING STRONG . . . TOGETHER

READ 1 CORINTHIANS 10:12-13

> *God is faithful; he will not let you*
> *be tempted beyond what you can bear.* – v. 13

I LOVE OLD-TIMEY, small-town ice cream parlors, the kind where every flavor is churned by hand and made only with local ingredients. There are always the typical flavors (chocolate, vanilla, etc.), but the other offerings are usually more exotic. Buttermilk pancakes, bacon, and eggs; strawberry honey balsamic and black pepper; and olive oil are only a few of the unusual offerings at one of my favorite ice cream spots. It can be hard deciding on a flavor to pick, and sometimes the offerings are so tempting that I cave and order a double—or even triple scoop! The worst part? I'm never immune from this ice cream decision-making paralysis . . . not even at the grocery store! In fact, leaving me in the ice cream aisle unattended for a long period of time can be quite dangerous.

But it's one thing to be tempted by a tantalizing array of ice cream flavors—it's quite another to be tempted by the devil himself.

Temptation is a real and difficult thing—not a single person who walks through this life can escape it. Even Jesus faced temptation! Hebrews 4:15 tells us that he was tempted in *every way* that we ourselves are. But like the incredible, infallible

Creator God that he is, Jesus stood strong. And now his Spirit is here in our hearts, walking with us and giving us the steadfastness we need to resist temptation.

Life is a journey of twists and turns, but our God doesn't just have the map. He *wrote* the map. He has a bird's-eye view of our life—our course, our direction. He alone is all the guidance we need. He understands when we face temptation, and he is walking alongside us, ready to reach out his loving hand and offer us the strength we need to stand against the enemy.

As Christians, we are called to reflect our Creator in every way. That means standing strong against temptation, but it also includes helping those around us do the same. Our friends, family members, and acquaintances struggle with temptation every day, but they don't have to go it alone. We can step out of our own comfort zone to act as an accountability partner or a source of encouragement. It doesn't matter whether we are unfamiliar with someone's struggles or have walked through the same valley. Just as Jesus brings people into our lives to help us keep our eyes on him, the Lord can use us to help others overcome temptation.

Unless, of course, the temptation in question comes in the form of a quadruple scoop of ice cream. At that point, resistance is futile!

Dear God, you know how hard it is to be tempted to sin. Help me to trust in you and stand firm against the lies of the devil. Give me strength today. Amen.

What are some things you are tempted to do? How can you replace those temptations with healthy, God-pleasing thoughts and actions? Do you know someone who is struggling to overcome a destructive habit or pattern of sin? How can you be a support to them during this time?

_____

_____

_____

_____

_____

_____

_____

_____

_____

_____

_____

_____

_____

DAY 4: SOUVENIR HUNT

READ DEUTERONOMY 7:6-15

> *God has chosen you out of all the peoples on the face of the earth to be his people, his treasured possession. - v. 6*

SOUVENIRS CAN SERVE as a tangible reminder of amazing memories from a trip. Sometimes they become our most treasured possessions. When my mom and I visited the Mediterranean, we collected several quintessentially European treasures—an embroidered linen handkerchief, centuries-old books, and even a bottle of French perfume. To this day, those small trinkets are an indispensable part of my daily life. I can't imagine *not* seeing the stack of books on my nightstand or smelling that perfume on special occasions.

Well, here's the thing—God sees us the same way. And no, I don't mean that he thinks of us all as a bunch of musty old books or handkerchiefs. I mean that he treasures us. Deeply. His love for us goes far beyond anything that we, as humans, can imagine or comprehend. Before we were ever born or even conceived, God knew us intimately. And he *loved us.*

How precious, then, God's people are—how worthy of our love and honor and respect! God crafted each of us for a special purpose, and he loves us with a depth that is beyond measure. So then we, too, should shower those around us with the same sort of Christlike love. Everyone we know is dearly beloved by God and created in his image. Are we treating them that way?

Sometimes it can be hard to remember that we're called to share the love of God with *everyone*—even particularly annoying people or those who have hurt us in the past. But when we step back and consider how fiercely the Lord loves us despite our flaws, it becomes easier to extend compassion to those around us. Jesus was willing to die for us when we were at our worst, so we can surely love others even at *their* worst.

No one is perfect, and we all have flaws that, at times, make us feel downright unlovable. But the Lord loves us all the time—and, with his help, we can do the same for others . . . even when it's hard.

Dear God, it's really amazing to know that I am loved by YOU! Thank you for seeking me out and chasing after my heart. Thank you for loving me and treating me as one of your own. I love you too, Lord. Please help me to show others the same kind of love you have shown me.

Is there someone in your life you've been struggling to show love to recently? Try making a list of their best attributes in a manner similar to the activity above. How does focusing on their positive qualities help you see them more like Jesus does?

_____

_____

_____

_____

_____

DAY 5: BEST TRIP EVER

READ EPHESIANS 2:4-9

> *By grace you have been saved through faith. And this is not*
> *your own doing; it is the gift of God.* ~ *v. 8 (ESV)*

WHEN I GRADUATED from high school, my mom gave me a wrapped gift. I opened it and found a plaque bearing a map of the world. And on the back of the plaque was a coupon: *Good for one "trip of a lifetime."* A million thoughts flew through my head as I considered the long list of destinations on my travel bucket list. Would I journey through Tokyo and the vibrant cities of Japan? Venture through the ancient wonders of the Middle East? Finally seize the chance to experience life on the East Coast of my home country? The excitement that flooded my heart then was dwarfed when I finally made my choice and booked a cruise that would take me around Europe for the first time in the fall. As long as I live, no gift can compare to that one.

But far better than any earthly gift is God's gift of eternal life! I know that can sound downright cheesy in some contexts.

But. It's. True.

My mom may have taken me on a trip that far exceeded my wildest dreams, but God has offered us all the true "trip of a lifetime"—all the way to his throne in heaven. And unlike most vacation experiences, life with Jesus will last forever.

God has given us this gift not because we deserve it but because he *loves* us. Our God is a God of kindness, mercy, and—above all—love. The gifts that he gives us are good because *he* is good. How blessed are we to have such an incredible Savior?

Not only has the Lord given us the gift of his love, but he has also equipped us with the tools we need to bless those around us. We might not be able to walk around handing out one-way tickets to heaven, but we *can* share a small bit of Christ's love with everyone we meet.

When we freely extend to others the goodness that we first received from the Lord, we are reflecting Christ's love for us. And who knows? The kindness and compassion that others experience through us might encourage them to take the first step on their own journey of a lifetime.

Wow, Lord! You continue to amaze me with your mighty power and love. Thank you for taking my sins to the cross so that I might have eternal life in you. Thank you for your grace and mercy, and for loving me no matter what I do. Please help me to show others that same kind of love and compassion each and every day. Amen.

God has given us so many gifts! Spend some time here thinking of and listing the other gifts he has blessed you with, then thank him for each of them individually. How could you use some of the gifts that God has given you to bless others in return?

_____

_____

_____

_____

_____

_____

_____

DAY 6: SUITCASE SUPPORT

READ JOHN 13:34-35

> *As I have loved you, so you must love one another. ~ v. 34*

THE TRAIN from Rome to Venice was cramped. Crowded. My suitcase was shoved in an upper compartment, wedged like a boulder against the roof of the train car. By the time my mom and I arrived at our station, we were exhausted from the trip and utterly overwhelmed at the thought of suitcase-wrangling—did I mention that our bags weighed more than seventy pounds? Each?!

I'll never forget the kindness of a woman we met that day. Though she spoke very little English and was no brawnier than I, she had no problem hauling down my mom's and my suitcases and giving me a friendly smile.

That small act of kindness meant the world to me.

We've talked a lot about God's love for us, but what about *our* love for *others*? If God's love for us has the power to touch hearts and transform lives, consider how our own kind words, deeds, and actions bless those around us!

This life isn't just about following our tour guide—it's also about building relationships with those we meet along the way. Our traveling companions, if you will. By greeting the people around us with big smiles and kind words—and going the extra mile to help them in times of need—we can ensure that we are blessing them with the same sweet gifts God has given us.

Dear God, thank you for the special people you've put in my life. Help me to show them your love day by day, and let me be a blessing to them as we travel through this world together.

....

Make a list of the people you know you'll be seeing today, then write down one small way you could show Christ's love to each of them.

_____

_____

_____

_____

_____

_____

_____

_____

_____

DAY 7: FROM DARK TO LIGHT

READ 1 THESSALONIANS 5:11-15

Encourage one another and build each other up. – v. 11

HAVE YOU EVER gotten up before dawn to travel somewhere—whether that's the top of a mountain or your own backyard—just to watch the sunrise? When you arrive, the area around you is cloaked in darkness; maybe even a few stars remain. Soon, a faint band of sunlight appears at the horizon, edged by darkened mountain peaks, and the stars fade into daylight.

Gossamer clouds swirl around you in an ever-changing kaleidoscope of color as the sun gets closer . . . closer . . . closer.

Finally.

The sun lifts its head above the horizon, flooding earth and sky in fresh, golden light. The landscape glows.

Light has come.

But it's not just the sun that is capable of such wonders. We, too, have the power to bring light to our corners of the world by encouraging the people around us. When we pay others compliments, offer words of wisdom, and invest in relationships, we bring about an even brighter transformation than a sunrise.

God uses sunrises to remind his children of his love, grace, and boundless creativity, and he uses *us* to spread his love to the people in our lives—our traveling companions. Let's encourage them every chance we get, whether through a compliment, a thoughtfully handwritten note, or a shoulder to cry on.

We may never know the darkness that those around us are walking through at any given time, but we can strive to bring them light no matter what. A small act of kindness or a compassionate word might seem simple to us, but it could be the one thing that keeps its recipient going for the rest of the day. Every act of goodness matters.

Our encouragement lights the world.

Thank you, Lord, for the opportunities you've given me to encourage others. Help me bring light to their lives . . . today and every day. Amen.

Encouraging others is a lifestyle! As you go about your day, be on the lookout for ways that you can compliment the people in your life. Even something small—like "Cute shoes!"—can go a long way toward brightening someone's day.

DAY 8: FORGETFUL FORGIVENESS

READ COLOSSIANS 3:12-14

Forgive as the Lord forgave you. ~ v. 13

WHEN I WAS in elementary school, my parents took me to Disneyland. It was every kid's dream—towering rides; an over-abundance of food (especially sugar); and all the mouse ears, princess costumes, and stuffed animals a girl could wish for. We faithfully put in our hours at the park each day, arriving at the crack of dawn and staying late to watch the fireworks. But one day, between the blistering sunshine, adrenaline-pumping thrill rides, and multiple sugar highs, I began to suffer from what I think of as "Disneyland burnout."

Suddenly, not even the "Happiest Place on Earth" could make me smile. I don't remember exactly what happened, but I can clearly recall sitting huffily on a bench in Downtown Disney one night as my dad gave me a "talk" about my attitude. But you know what?

The rest of my memories from that trip are filled with

pirate-themed rides, encounters with my favorite princesses, and mouse-shaped waffles. After our talk, my dad completely forgave me. He was willing to look past my crabbiness that night. Even though I'd made a mistake, he didn't hold it against me for the rest of the trip. In fact, he forgot about it!

So too does our heavenly Father lovingly forgive our sins. The Bible assures us that, when we confess our wrongdoings to the Lord, he is quick to cast aside our iniquity and replace wrath with grace. But it shouldn't stop there! We should be fast to forgive others when they hurt us, like my dad was so quick to forgive me.

Jesus sacrificed so much in order to pardon our sins, and he did so freely—willingly. Our sins hurt him more than we could ever know, but he is still faithful and just to forgive us. When we show others that same sort of forgiveness, we can be a bright, beautiful blessing in their lives.

And you know what? When we forgive others, we can turn anywhere in the world into the *real* "Happiest Place on Earth."

Dear God, thank you for forgiving me even though I don't deserve it! Please help me to show the same kind of love and grace to others. Give me the strength to be kind and to forgive—even when it hurts.

How can you extend forgiveness to someone in your life today?

_____

_____

_____

_____

_____

_____

_____

DAY 9: PARENTAL TRAVEL AGENTS

READ EPHESIANS 6:1-9

Children, obey your parents in the Lord, for this is right. - v. 1

MY MOM CAN make any decision in approximately ten seconds flat. Despite my love of playing "travel agent," I've learned to sit back and let her make the final call on most of our vacation decisions instead of trying to singlehandedly micromanage every step of the trip. (I have a hard time picking something to eat off a menu, let alone choosing where to go for dinner!) Even if my mom's ideas are different from what I'd originally anticipated, they're usually far better than what I could have come up with on my own.

Just like my mom has a sort of sixth sense when it comes to making amazing travel plans, our parents generally have our best interests in mind. But even when they make mistakes (because hey—we're all human), God calls us to honor them with our obedience. That also means we need to honor our grandparents and other relatives, foster parents, teachers, and even family friends. All the people in our life who mentor and guide us deserve our respect.

It's easy to want to go our own way and ignore the advice of older friends, family members, and parents, but that isn't how God wants us to act. We wouldn't travel halfway across the world to explore a new country and then go against everything our tour guide suggested. So why would we disobey those who love and care about us, and who are further along in the journey?

When we listen to our elders and show them respect, we are not only blessing these people in our lives; we're also mirroring the sort of relationship the Lord desires with his people. Of course, our parents are human too—sometimes they mess up and make mistakes. In fact, there might be occasions when we have to go against what our parents have planned for us in order to stay on the path Christ has set us on. Oftentimes, however, our parents have great plans for us—amazing hopes and dreams for our future. Obeying them honors our heavenly Father, too—and that's always the best way to live!

God, thank you for the people you've put into my life to help guide me as I grow in you and make difficult decisions. Help me to obey and honor them as they teach me the ways I should go. Most of all, thank you for being my heavenly Father and for always having a plan for my life. I love you, Lord. Amen.

Who are some of your earthly "travel guides"? Make a list of them here—parents, grandparents, teachers, etc.—and consider how you can honor and obey them today.

_____

_____

_____

_____

_____

_____

DAY 10: DIRECTIONALLY CHALLENGED

READ PROVERBS 13

> *Walk with the wise and become wise,*
> *for a companion of fools suffers harm. ~ v. 20*

—○○○—

I'M WHAT YOU WOULD CALL directionally challenged. I can be holding a GPS in my hands, listening to its directions, and still get someone on the completely wrong track! Needless to say, I'm a terrible backseat driver, and people know to disregard my navigational assistance whenever I'm riding shotgun.

My bad directions can turn any road trip into a dead end in a matter of minutes, and hanging out with "bad company" can get us off course in our spiritual lives just as quickly. It's great to spend time with unbelievers and act as a witness to them, but when we spend all of our time around those who don't share our values and beliefs, we can make ourselves susceptible to the devil's evil rerouting scheme.

Pressure from our peers to engage in gossip or treat others unkindly can make us second-guess the road map God has given us. If we're not careful, we end up tossing our God-given directions aside and going blindly along with whatever the world tells us is right for us. As we continue down the route that God has set out for us, we need to be vigilant—watchful—against such temptations. One way we can do that is to make sure that our traveling companions won't steer us down the wrong path.

By fostering friendships with those who share our values, we're not only protecting ourselves from the devil's misdirection; we're also giving ourselves a better chance at living a life that pleases God. When we walk down the road of life with friends who can encourage us, challenge us, and pray for us, we can be sure that they'll call us out if we get off track.

Who am I kidding? We're all going to take some wrong turns now and again, but when we have a network of supportive, Jesus-loving friends in our corner, it's a whole lot easier to find our way back to the path we've been called to walk.

God, I want to pick the right traveling companions for my life's journey. Please help me to connect with others and build friendships that glorify and honor you. Amen.

Invite a friend to start working through a Bible study or book of devotions with you! As you read, text back and forth or meet up once a week to chat about what you've learned. Together, you can help each other follow God's directions.

bonus adventure: a date with God

You're Invited

when: WHENEVER YOU WANT

where: YOUR BACKYARD, A COZY ARMCHAIR BY THE WINDOW, OR A NEARBY PARK

what: A SPECIAL OPPORTUNITY FOR YOU TO GROW YOUR RELATIONSHIP WITH THE LORD . . . AND MAYBE OTHERS, TOO!

the details: DURING THE REMAINDER OF YOUR TIME SPENT TRAVELING THROUGH THE PAGES OF THIS BOOK, YOU'RE GOING TO FIND SEVERAL MINI-ADVENTURES— OPPORTUNITIES FOR YOU TO GET AWAY WITH THE LORD, DO SOME JOURNALING, AND EVEN MAKE A TASTY SNACK.

It's important for us to take time to nurture our relationships with friends and family, and it's equally important that we set aside a special time to grow closer to the Lord . . . but that can be hard to do! Morning devotions are great, but sometimes we yawn our way through them. With this activity, you will have an opportunity to spend some serious quality time with our Lord and Savior—a "date," if you will.

Pick a time when you'll have a few uninterrupted hours. Whip up a loaf of this quick, easy, and *delicious* French bread (it's great by itself or with meat, cheese, and fruit for a true Parisian feast!) before settling down for some time with the Lord.

Oh là là French Bread

1½ CUPS WARM WATER

1 TABLESPOON HONEY

1½ TEASPOONS SALT

1 TABLESPOON ACTIVE DRY YEAST

4 CUPS FLOUR

¼ CUP BUTTER, BROWNED (SEE NOTE)

BUTTER FOR SERVING

1. Combine water, honey, salt, and yeast in a bowl and let sit for about ten minutes. At this point, the top of the mixture should look bubbly and foamy.

2. When the yeast has "bloomed" (aka started making those bubbles), knead in the flour until the dough is no longer sticky. (If it's still sticky once the flour is mixed in, you might need to add about ½ cup more.)

3. Turn the dough out onto a parchment-lined baking sheet and form it into a loaf. Cover the loaf and let sit in a warm place while you preheat the oven to 400° F.

4. Once the dough has rested for about twenty minutes, cut several slits in the top of the loaf. Brush the loaf all over with melted browned butter (reserve any left over) before baking for 16–20 minutes. Brush with any remaining browned butter and serve warm with (you guessed it) more butter!

NOTE: To brown butter, place in a pan and heat until melted and caramel-colored. It may start to smoke a little, and that's okay! Just keep a close eye on it so that the caramelization doesn't turn into *burnt*.

To jazz up your presentation, sprinkle your butter pat with sea salt, chopped fresh herbs (I love rosemary and, surprisingly, lavender), or both! After all, compound butters are *très chic*!

Although this loaf can comfortably serve one (at least, I like to think that it can . . .), it's really meant to be shared. Consider extending your date with the Lord by inviting family and friends to share in good food and fellowship. Lay out some fruit and cheese, play some quiet instrumental or worship music, and work through the following questions together. On the flip side, you can make this a super special time just between you and God. (That way there's more bread for you too!)

THINGS TO THINK ON

- How am I encouraging others to chase wholeheartedly after their Savior?

- Am I a witness to those around me who might not know Jesus?

- How do my relationships with others inspire me in my own walk with the Lord?

- How is my relationship with Jesus? Have I been devoting ample time to him, or has he become more of an afterthought?

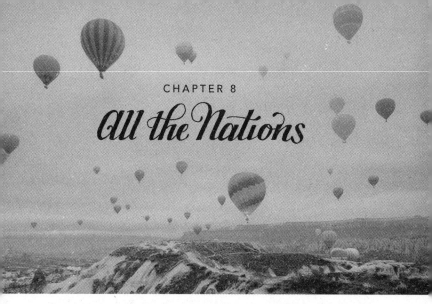

CHAPTER 8

All the Nations

DAY 1: TRAVELING COMPANIONS

READ MATTHEW 28:16-20

> *Therefore go and make disciples of all nations. – v. 19*

WHEN I TRAVEL, it's almost second nature for me to make new friends along the way. There's something about living on a ship or prowling around a relatively small island with a group of like-minded people that just seems to foster friendships. In fact, I've met some of my closest friends on cruise ships!

The funny thing is, I'm not typically the kind of person who bursts out the front door every morning intent on making new friends. I'm an introvert. But knowing that we're all sailing aboard a ship, walking along a tropical beach, or exploring a medieval city for the same reason—to learn, grow, explore, and quench our wanderlust—makes it easy to form lifelong relationships with people who were, just days before, perfect strangers. The same is true in life. Other than our family, it's up to us to pick and choose our "traveling companions," so to speak.

But God doesn't simply want us to go through life making friends and building relationships with others. Yes, that's an important part of our journey here on earth, but he has also called us to a higher purpose. During the famous Great Commission passage in the Bible—today's featured reading—Jesus commanded his followers to go out into all the nations and win others' hearts for him.

That's a big undertaking, and, while it can feel intimidating, it's also exciting. The Lord himself desires to work through us and our lives to draw others to Christ. He wants us to join with him to bring about his Kingdom here on earth!

Now, if you're on the introvert spectrum like I am, this command can be a little overwhelming. I mean, if you're not a fan of making small talk with the barista at your favorite coffee shop, how much harder does it sound to go out into *all nations* and share the Good News of Jesus?

We all have different strengths, and not all of us are meant for life on the mission field. However, we are all given a million little chances to show Jesus to others. Every single day.

As we journey through this chapter together, we'll learn more about how the Lord designed us to reflect his love to each and every person we meet. We'll discover how to live a life that inspires others to become intimately acquainted with their Creator. We'll find out how to show Christ's love in such a way that, whether we speak his name in words or actions, others will see him in us and maybe even become fellow traveling companions on our journey of faith.

Dear Lord, the command you have given us is a big one, and it can be daunting at times. I want to do your will in my life, and I know that includes showing your love to others. Please help me to live in a way that draws others' eyes to you. Amen.

....

Write down that key verse! Then consider . . . How do you feel about the Great Commission? Is it exciting or intimidating? Do you feel cut out for the task of helping lead others to Christ? If not, use this space to ask the Lord to give you guidance, wisdom, and courage as you seek to proclaim the goodness of his name.

DAY 2: THE LANGUAGE WE SPEAK

READ JOHN 13:31-35

> *By this everyone will know that you are my disciples,*
> *if you love one another. ~ v. 35*

WHEN I WAS in France, I took a day trip into the seaside town of Nice and spent the afternoon rambling around Vieux Nice, the city's old town. Cobbled streets and alleyways led to bustling city squares lined with red-striped tents overflowing with fresh flowers, handmade soaps, and artisan bread. Vieux Nice is built into the side of a hill, so it was steep going as slanted stairways led from one street to the next. The town was filled to overflowing—and *everyone* was speaking French!

Considering I know how to say little more than *bonjour, oui,* and *s'il vous plaît,* it was easy to feel lost amid the fast-paced chatter of the locals and the completely unintelligible street signs. My mom and I chatted away—in English, of course—as we explored, but imagine our delight when a couple spoke to us out of the blue.

"Are you from America?" they asked in perfect English.

We ended up having a wonderful conversation—in English!—outside a little French fabric shop. As it turns out, the couple were American expats, and, though they'd been living in Nice for a couple of years, they still didn't speak much French. To say they were excited to hear someone speaking English was an understatement.

Just like that couple in France could tell that my mom and I were Americans from the language we spoke, the people around you and me can tell we are Christ followers through the words that *we* speak. Now, this doesn't mean we have to go around spouting churchy words and talking about sin, salvation, and repentance all the time. These things have their place, and there are definitely times for us to boldly share the gospel. However, we can also share Jesus simply by building people up with kind words and loving encouragement. Whether we tell others about Jesus directly by sharing his Word or by simply extending kindness to them, we can give the world a glimpse of the God who lives in us.

By offering words of care and love to all those we come into contact with—whether that means our best friend or a stranger on the street—we are showing whose Kingdom we belong to. When we take care to speak words that are good, true, pure, and lovely (basically everything you read in Philippians 4:8), we demonstrate that we are different from the rest of the world. Through Christ, we have new hearts and minds. We have peace. We have joy.

And when we show that peace and joy to others through kind words and loving deeds, we could be giving them their first true hint of God's Kingdom.

Dear Lord, thank you for giving me the opportunity to show your love to others through my words and actions. Help me to view each and every encounter as a chance to be a witness for you. Amen.

Keep an eye out for opportunities to show Christ's love to others today. Then write about some of the ways you did so below.

_____

_____

_____

_____

_____

_____

DAY 3: A REASON FOR LIVING

READ 1 PETER 3:13-18

> *Always be prepared to give an answer to everyone who asks you to give the reason for the hope that you have. ~ v. 15*

"WHAT'S YOUR REASON for living?"

When a zip line tour guide half-jokingly asked me that question hundreds of feet above the Hawaiian rain forest, my tongue nearly stuck in my throat. I was the last one in my group to fly across the chasm. The guide and I were alone on the other side. Yeah, this guy was a jokester, and I knew he probably wasn't expecting a serious answer, but even so, just before I jumped off the platform to begin my flight through the open air, I gave him the best answer I knew.

"I'm a Christian, so I want to serve the Lord in all I do."

Now, knowing me, my real answer was probably considerably less eloquent (and more rambling) than that, but I knew deep in my heart that I couldn't hide my love for Jesus. Even in this moment—high above a tropical rain forest, strapped into a zip-lining harness, talking to a guy I'd met only a few hours before—I knew I wanted to boldly tell the truth about the God who lives in me.

So I did.

Being a witness for Christ isn't always a matter of going on a mission trip, donating a bunch of money to a charitable cause, or volunteering at a local homeless shelter. In fact, being a witness is a lot less about *what* you do and a lot more about *how* you do it.

Let's face it—if I can share Jesus with a zip line tour guide in the middle of a tropical jungle, we can all be witnesses for Christ amid the day-to-day and the mundane. By showing joy—the kind of joy that comes from the Lord—to everyone we meet, we're planting the smallest of seeds in their hearts. And then, when they ask us about that joy we possess, we can be ready with the answer of a lifetime. *It's all Jesus.*

Dear heavenly Father, I know you are the reason for the joy that I have here on this earth. Please help me to show that joy to others, and give me the words to speak when they ask me about you. Amen.

The next time someone asks you about the reason for your contagious laugh, big smile, or endless compassion, point to Jesus and give him the glory. You never know how a simple mention of his name could change another person's life!

DAY 4: A LASTING IMPACT

READ ROMANS 12:3-8

> *We have different gifts, according to*
> *the grace given to each of us. ~ v. 6*

I'LL NEVER FORGET the last dinner I ever had aboard a European cruise ship. For the past two weeks, I'd dined aboard the ship, getting to know my tablemates—those beloved "cruise grand-parents"—so well that I nearly considered them family. That very last evening, as we prepared to say farewell, my emotions were already running high.

And *then* . . . one of them pulled out a gift. It wasn't wrapped (we were on a cruise ship, after all!) or extravagant, but it touched my heart nonetheless. To this day, that French olive-wood spoon from my European friends has helped me stir countless pots of spaghetti sauce and stew. Though some might consider a spoon simple and insignificant, it meant the world to me.

Just as that small gift touched my heart more than my friends could ever know, our actions have the power to dramatically impact lives for God's Kingdom. The Lord has blessed each and every one of us with special talents—a selection of which are listed in today's reading—that we can use to bless people around the world.

All of us have been called to be living, breathing witnesses for the Lord. Some will leave their home countries to go into the world and preach the gospel, but others have quieter callings. Some of the gifts God has given us are meant to be used behind the scenes, but that doesn't make them any less special.

A long hug on a hard day can often mean more than a swiftly spoken Bible verse. A smile on a street corner can speak more truth than even the greatest sermons. A "just because" text, card, or gift is worth so much more than it costs.

God has given each of us the unique ability to serve others in a variety of ways, and we can use our spiritual gifts not only to bring him glory but also to encourage others and point them toward him. Our gifts can even open the door for us to share more openly about the true and wonderful love of Christ. We simply have to be ready and waiting for those opportunities to arise—and bold enough to seize them when they come around.

Dear Lord Jesus, thank you for blessing me with so many unique gifts. Help me to use them to serve others and turn their eyes toward you. Amen.

Which of the spiritual gifts listed in today's passage (prophesying, serving, teaching, encouraging, giving, leading, and showing mercy) resonate with you the most? How can you use that gift to help others draw near to the Lord?

_____

_____

_____

_____

_____

_____

DAY 5: FREE UPGRADES

READ MARK 10:35-45

> *The Son of Man did not come to be served, but to serve,*
> *and to give his life as a ransom for many. ~ v. 45*

HAVE YOU EVER tried to get a free upgrade? I know I have! There are a thousand little tips and tricks on the internet for how to get free upgrades *everywhere*—on airplanes, in hotels, and even at restaurants. (Pro tip: many chain restaurants will give you a free appetizer or dessert just for signing up for their email list!)

The best free upgrade I ever scored was in Las Vegas. My family took a weekend trip to escape the cold Oregon rain, explore the outlandish resorts, and eat a lot of really good food, and I tried out one of those free upgrade hacks when we checked into our hotel. Sure enough, my family was granted a room with a stunning view of not only the city lights but also the mountains in the distance.

It can be fun to see what kind of upgrades we can score when we're traveling, but have you ever tried to "upgrade" your position in heaven by being extra good simply for the sake of trying to win an additional share of the Lord's favor? James and John did just that in today's passage—and it didn't go too well.

As Christians, we have been called not to be served but to *serve*. Jesus himself knelt before his disciples to wash their feet—their dirty, grimy, smelly, mucky feet! The apostles devoted their lives to serving others and proclaiming Christ's name throughout the world. Missionaries today give up the comfort and security of their own countries—their own homes—in order to bring others the Good News of Jesus.

Many of us (myself included!) spend way too much time searching for those "free upgrades." We hope that if we live a "perfect" life (spoiler alert—nobody's perfect), God will pile extra blessings upon us. Instead of taking our relationship with Christ for granted or viewing our position in heaven as a prize to be won, let's follow Jesus' lead. Our Savior—the only One who could be both man and God—didn't come to earth in a triumph of trumpet blasts. He came quietly. He came for us—for me and for you. He gave up his glory to show us just how loved we are.

Maybe today we can do the same.

Lord, your love for us is unbelievable. You brought people to yourself by giving them the gift of your presence, not by sitting on a golden throne. Help me to touch lives for you not by trying to impress others but by laying down my own life to serve them. Amen.

How can you use your everyday experiences and encounters to bless others and point them to Jesus?

DAY 6: WORTH THE COST

READ 2 TIMOTHY 2:8-14

> *Therefore I endure everything for the sake of the elect, that they too may obtain the salvation that is in Christ Jesus. ~ v. 10*

WHAT'S THE LONGEST you've ever been in the car at one time?

When I was little, my family made several pilgrimages to Disneyland—and we'd tackle the entire eight-hundred-mile drive in a single day. That meant twelve-plus hours in the car.

If you've ever driven down the California interstate, you probably know just how *boring* that landscape is. Endless fields. Dust devils. Utter nothingness.

I'm not going to lie—those car rides were brutal, but it was all worth it when we finally pulled up in front of the "Happiest Place on Earth." Even at a young age, I was willing to endure the seemingly endless road trip because I knew it would pay off in the end.

How much more worthwhile must it have felt, then, for the apostle Paul to watch thousands of people come to Christ, despite the suffering that he endured in prison. Rather than spending a day strapped into a car seat and playing the license plate game for the millionth time, Paul spent more than five years in prison throughout his life. And yet, even when he was suffering, he did it with joy and gladness—because he knew that the Lord would use these trials to point others back to him.

When we walk through difficult times, it's easy to develop an "Are-we-there-yet?" complex. After all, trials of any type are *tiring*. But sometimes the Lord allows challenges into our lives to shape us and mold us as his followers. Sometimes those trials make us stronger witnesses for him.

God always has a plan and a way to turn even our darkest nights into his greatest testimonies. But when we walk through the fire and emerge unscathed, is it enough to simply praise the Lord for his goodness? Or does he have other plans for us—plans for something more?

When we overcome seemingly insurmountable trials, there are people in our lives who would no doubt love to hear about it. Why not use these incredible stories as opportunities to share about God's goodness with everyone . . . even those who might not yet know him? By speaking boldly about the incredible things the Lord has done for us, we are not only giving God the glory he deserves but also sharing the Good News with others—a win-win!

One thing is for sure—when we endure trials, we become living testaments to God's goodness and faithfulness. And *that* could be the very thing that leads someone to salvation.

Dear God, sometimes I don't know why life turns out the way it does. Sometimes I feel trapped—like this isn't the way my life should be. Help me look to you even when I don't understand. Let me live for you, even in difficult times, so that I can continue to be a witness to others in all that I do. Amen.

What is something difficult you're dealing with during this leg of your journey? How might the Lord be using you as a witness for him even in the midst of your hardships?

_____

_____

_____

_____

_____

_____

DAY 7: AMBASSADORS FOR CHRIST

READ 2 CORINTHIANS 5:11-21

We are therefore Christ's ambassadors. - v. 20

—○○○—

HAVE YOU EVER thought about being an exchange student?

When I was in high school, I would sometimes fantasize about traveling across the ocean to spend a semester in one country or another. For a while I dreamed of immersing myself in the culture of Japan; then it was Italy. I also considered Peru or Morocco for a while. And then, just as quickly as my fantasy began, it was inevitably snuffed out by the realization that I would be *homesick*. Like, really homesick. (Because, for as much as I love to travel, I prefer not to do it alone.)

At the same time, I know that there are a ton of people who thrive in an exchange-student setting. They rise to the challenge of adjusting to life in a new place and enjoy representing their home country while overseas. In a way, they're like an ambassador.

What exactly is an ambassador? Ambassadors as we know them are diplomats who travel to other countries in order to make sure their homeland is well represented. They go to great lengths to "show off" their country and make a good impression on the people around them.

But being an ambassador isn't just for exchange students or diplomats—it's for you and me too! The Lord has called us to be *his* representatives, to spend every one of our days on this earth showing others what his Kingdom is like. Whether it's through a softly spoken message of kindness or a bold declaration of the gospel, there are chances every day for us to tell others about the Good News.

The Lord has many purposes for each of us, but one of the most important is to share him with others. When we became Christians, we also became equipped to help other people find salvation through Christ.

God has given us the tools we need to be ambassadors wherever we are. The specifics of that role will vary depending on where we live and the people we interact with on a day-to-day basis, but that just makes our job all the more important.

So today, when you step out onto the sidewalk or walk into your first class at school, remember to view the world not as a "local" but as an ambassador for Christ—an envoy from his Kingdom. Let's treat people with his kindness, love, and mercy. Let's show others what it looks like to trust in him. Let's seize every opportunity to tell others about the goodness of our God.

Dear Lord, thank you for allowing me to be an ambassador for you. Help me to not take this position lightly but to use it to speak your truth to the people around me. Show me how to do that, and give me the strength and courage to speak out and touch hearts for you. Amen.

....

Just like you might notice a lot of differences between your hometown and a different country, there are many differences between this world and God's Kingdom. What are some of the main differences? How can we—as Christ's ambassadors—show others the glories found in him?

_____

_____

_____

_____

_____

_____

DAY 8: LIGHT OF THE WORLD

READ MATTHEW 5:14-16

Let your light so shine . . . that they may see your good works and glorify your Father in heaven. ~ v. 16 (NKJV)

FOR WHATEVER REASON, the cruise ship didn't depart from the French port of Villefranche-sur-Mer on time. Instead of sailing at sunset, the ship stayed put far into the evening hours. Throughout the night, my mom, my friends, and I frequently stole peeks out the ship's picture windows. The hilly coastline, which had been dotted with quaint cottages and random jumbles of storefronts and apartments during the day, now fairly glittered with lamplight. I've carried that picture of the French coastline in a special place in my heart ever since, and it's what comes to mind when I read the famous "light of the world" passage in Matthew.

The Bible tells us that *we* are like that French town on the hillside. Our light shines before others just as the streetlights twinkled and winked and shone so that they were visible even from the harbor. As Christians, we were not created to be quiet about our faith. We are not meant to hide away or to keep the beautiful truth of the gospel to ourselves.

Instead, Jesus Christ implores us to live life boldly—for *him*!

When we live for the Lord, we stand out. While sometimes standing out is considered a bad thing (like when you're wearing—gasp!—flip-flops in France . . .), it's an honor to stand out as a Christ follower. We should earnestly *desire* this sort of set-apart-ness. There's nothing better in the world than being able to tell someone that you're a Christian through both actions *and* words.

I didn't need to check my location on a GPS to know that my ship was still safely anchored in the Villefranche marina because I could still see the city lights on the hill. Likewise, we shouldn't need to loudly proclaim the name of Jesus for people to know that we are his followers. Some forms of witnessing start slowly at first—a gentle, flickering light that catches the attention of others. And then, as they begin to draw closer, we can open our hearts and share all that the Lord has done for us. Words of friendship and acts of kindness can pave the way for bold declarations and invitations to follow Jesus as we continually shine our light. The flicker of Christ's love is fanned into a flame.

If we are truly living *in* the Lord and *for* the Lord, we already have everything we need to share him with others. His power is within us, giving us the courage to loudly proclaim his name as well as the ability to show others the same sort of love that he shows us daily. This sort of wild, reckless, passionate love might manifest itself differently in each of us, but we have all been called to proclaim the gift of God's grace.

Every second.

Every day.

Dear heavenly Father, what a gift it is to have your love living in me. Please let it shine out of me in everything I do. Help me to honor you with my life and represent you as a true city on a hill. Help me to live in a way that brings you glory and points others in your direction. In your name I pray, amen.

....

If you're a naturally shy person, do one thing today to really shine for Christ! Even if you're more extroverted, find a way to step outside your comfort zone and shine your light just a little bit brighter.

DAY 9: CALLED TO SERVE

READ 1 PETER 4:1-11

Above all, love each other deeply. - v. 8

IF THERE'S SOMETHING I LOVE even more than traveling, it's eating! Fortunately, these two activities often go hand in hand. There's nothing quite like getting a little dressed up and going out to dinner.

Going to a restaurant—especially a fancy one!—can be a whole adventure in and of itself. Sometimes it isn't even about the food so much as it is the *ambience*. And the service! The best restaurants don't just serve delectable dishes and have elegant, white-clothed tables. No, a truly fantastic restaurant has a whole team of people working to make dining there an experience.

Waiters and waitresses at these fine-dining establishments place your napkin on your lap for you, "crumb" the table in between courses to keep things looking just so, and generally make everyone feel like royalty during their visit. They treat every customer with kindness and compassion. They make sure everyone feels cared for—*seen*.

Now, either I could turn this into an elaborate, heavy-handed metaphor about our own duties as Christians (if we want to give others the Bread of Life, we must do so with a smile), or I could be a bit more subtle. Sadly, subtlety has never really been the name of my game, so I'm going to go the more direct route.

Because honestly, we all *have* been called to serve. Today's passage touches on that, reminding us that we should cheerfully provide hospitality and use our unique abilities to bless others. As Christians, we have an incredible gift to offer the world—the salvation found in Jesus Christ! When offering this gift to others, we must take care to show him off in the best light possible.

Just like the food at a restaurant tastes a hundred times better when it's served with a smile (have you noticed this?!), we have the opportunity to shine a powerful light on our Savior each and every time we interact with others. We have been called to evangelize, yes, but we've learned this week that *evangelism* doesn't always equal *preaching*.

Simply by serving others, we can show them the love of God. By offering a stranger a smile or giving a friend a shoulder to cry on, we are fulfilling the law of Christ. As today's passage says, we are to love each other *deeply*—not just on a surface level, not just when we feel like it.

We are called to love everyone—friends and family, yes, but also every person God has placed in our lives. We were created to show them the same fierce, passionate love that God has for us. We are to live our lives with a heart not just for Christ but also for his people—and that means loving and serving them always.

So as we offer those around us the Bread of Life, let's not do it halfheartedly or begrudgingly. Let's do it with joy—with love and care and compassion. In doing this, we can give everyone around us a taste of the five-star treatment that they'll receive when they put their faith and trust in God.

Dear Lord Jesus, it's impossible for me to share your love with others if I do not love them myself. Help me to honor others in word and in deed and to show them the same kind of love that you have shown me. Amen.

How can you love others today?

_____

_____

_____

_____

_____

_____

DAY 10: ONE WAY IN

READ JOHN 14:5-14

> *I am the way and the truth and the life. No one comes*
> *to the Father except through me. ~ v. 6*

CLOSE YOUR EYES for a moment and picture this.

You're standing at the prow of a speedboat as it pulls into a small, crescent-shaped harbor. All around you bob small fishing vessels with words in unfamiliar alphabets splashed across their hulls. When you hop off the boat, you stroll down a narrow stretch of pavement before turning onto a small, bustling street lined with cafés and souvenir shops. The smell of parmesan, basil, and oregano hangs thick in the air, and craftsmen hawk their wares—handmade sandals, locally made olive oil . . . the options are endless.

Do you know where you are?

You've just stepped foot on the island of Capri, which means you're in the heart of Marina Grande, the main port city of one of Italy's most beloved islands.

If you're visiting Capri, it's a guarantee that you'll experience the magic of Marina Grande—it's the only way for most tourists to access this stunning Italian destination.

As one must first visit Marina Grande before taking the funicular (or the stairs . . . phew!) up to Capri Town, we also must first trust in Jesus Christ and his leading before we can come to the Father.

Without the raw, pure love of God, none of us can be saved. That also means we alone are not responsible for anyone else's salvation. Yes, God has gifted us with the ability and opportunity to speak to others about his Son—to show them Jesus' love and goodness—but the true miracle of salvation happens through Christ alone.

So, as we do go out into the world, striving to spread peace and joy and love and make disciples of all nations, we must hold tight and fast to this truth: salvation comes from the Lord. We are the tools in his hands as he works miracles that bring people to him.

And what a privilege that is.

Lord, without you none of us would be saved. Thank you for your grace and kindness and goodness. Please use me as an instrument in your hands to direct people's hearts and minds to you and you alone. Amen.

....

Ask God to show you one person who needs to hear the Good News. Make a committed (and prayerful!) effort to show them Christ's love through your words and deeds in the coming week.

bonus adventure: be random

Today, let's reach out and share God's great love with others through some random acts of kindness! Whether your day is full of bustle or looks a little boring, there are *always* ways we can spread the love of Jesus—wherever we are! Choose a few random acts of kindness from the list below to carry out in the next couple of days, or expand the list with your own ideas. No matter what you choose to do, just know that you'll be richly blessing others with your generous heart and kind spirit.

• Pay it forward—it's easy and fun! For example, you could leave a couple of dollars and a note instructing the finder to "treat themselves" in the toy aisle of your local dollar store or offer to pay for coffee for the person behind you in line at a café.

• Take some sidewalk chalk and write Bible verses, encouraging quotes, or sweet messages on a friend's driveway or the sidewalk.

• Buy a gift card to a local restaurant (not a chain—support small businesses!), and tape it to a park bench with a kind note for whoever finds it first.

- Buy a bouquet of cheery balloons and tie them to a neighbor's mailbox.

- Write a letter—yes, a *real* letter—to a faraway (or nearby!) friend or family member. They'll love to hear from you!

- Grab a pad of sticky notes and write heartfelt notes or timely Bible verses for your mom, dad, or sibling— then stick them all over the house in areas where your family members will be sure to find them.

- Tie a bag of cookies or other goodies to a friend or family member's car door handle while they're at school or work.

- Buy a pack of washable window markers and write encouraging messages or Bible verses on bathroom mirrors at your school or home.

CHAPTER 9

The Final Step

DAY 1: PLANNING AHEAD

READ JEREMIAH 29:10-14

> *"I know the plans I have for you," declares*
> *the LORD, "plans to prosper you and not to harm you,*
> *plans to give you hope and a future." ~ v. 11*

I LOVE HAVING A PLAN—especially when I go places. I like to have my itinerary all dialed in, flight times and numbers memorized, and everything on my packing list neatly checked off before I set out on an adventure. I plan what I'll do, where I'll go . . . sometimes even what I'll eat. Because why not? Plans are great! (So I say up until it comes time to follow through with them, at which point I always remember that I far prefer to live on the edge.)

Plans *can* be pretty fantastic, but in reality, our clumsy human intentions pale before God's great design for our life. All of the dreams in the world that we can chase are nothing compared to the Lord's incredible, holy, powerful plan.

We might have come up with an entire road map for our future—go to college, get married, etc.—but God is our ultimate Navigator, our eternal Guide. Sometimes our plans line up with the Lord's, especially when we're delighting ourselves in him and allowing him to fill our hearts with dreams and goals, but sometimes God's plans for us are vastly different.

When times like that come—when the Lord puts the brakes on what we thought was a full-steam-ahead adventure, or when God pushes us out of our nice, cozy comfort zone—we have to cling to words like the ones found in this chapter's key verse. The Lord spoke to his people through the prophet Jeremiah when they were in the midst of an unplanned and unprecedented crisis. The Israelites had been taken captive by the Babylonians, and suddenly *nothing* was the way it should be.

But even in the midst of this great unrest, when fear blanketed the hearts of God's people, our Creator wasn't afraid. Because he had a plan. And this plan wasn't for desolation or destruction, as the Israelites might have thought, but for hope. A future.

During this journey of life, we will all have to travel down rough parts of the road. They're unpaved. Sometimes even dangerous. But these challenges are all part of God's plan. As daughters of the King, we each play an irreplaceable role in his

Kingdom. The path that God has mapped out for us might not always be easy, but it will always be right.

As we embark on an adventure through this last chapter today, let's hold fast to the words in today's key verse—words like *hope* and *future*. Whether we have a clear idea of the road God wants us to walk down or we're just taking things step by step, one at a time, let's be reminded in the coming days that the Lord's plans for us are always better than our own.

They really are.

Dear Lord, you are so amazing! I don't know everything that you have planned for me in this life, but I'm so excited to discover what's in store. Thank you for your goodness, your faithfulness, and for providing a road map through your Word. Amen.

....

What good plans for your life have you seen the Lord revealing lately? Write about some of them here. (And then write down this chapter's key verse and add it to your collection!)

_____

_____

_____

_____

_____

DAY 2: SERVANT OR FAMILY?

READ JOHN 15:9-17

I have called you friends. ~ v. 15

ON CRUISE SHIPS, staff members go above and beyond to create an amazing experience for guests. I'll never forget one time on a cruise when room service delivered a tray of chocolate-covered strawberries to our room, complete with an apology note—and all because they'd accidentally put yolks in my egg-white omelet!

The service staff aboard that cruise ship knew how to make everyone onboard feel special and cared for and . . . well . . . almost *loved*. By the time I disembarked a couple weeks later, I had tears in my eyes as I bid the staff members—many of whom had come to feel like family—farewell.

In today's passage, we are commanded to serve and show love to others in the same way that Jesus Christ has loved us. But even though we're called to serve God and others, we're not to be known as mere servants. We aren't simply asked to do the Lord's work; we're invited to know him intimately. On a level so deep that we become his *friends*.

This passage promises us that God will guide us when we are in close relationship with him. We weren't randomly created, then left to chance or fate. Instead, our Father crafted us to enjoy intimacy with him as he reveals his will in each of our lives.

We will grow closer to the Lord the longer we live for him. And our love for God will deepen as we become more and more aware of the depth of his love for us. As our Father continues to reveal his will, we will come to trust and rely on him more and more.

God's will is an incredible thing. That he actually has a plan for us is amazing enough by itself, but the fact that he is continually speaking to us through his Word is something special.

The precious relationship that we have with our Father is what defines Christianity. While other religions hinge on servitude, our faith finds its foundation not simply in our works but in *love* and *faith*.

The love of a Father for his children, a Master for his servant.

One friend for another.

Dear God, what a privilege and honor it is not only to serve you but to love you as one dear friend loves another. Thank you for the gift of getting to know you and your heart so well. Thank you for your love. Amen.

....

How do you feel about your relationship with the Lord? Have you experienced the sort of intimate friendship described in John 15, or are you still searching for that kind of relationship with your Creator? What would it look like for you to grow closer to Christ?

DAY 3: CHRIST FIRE

READ 2 TIMOTHY 1:6-14

> *Fan into flame the gift of God, which is in you. – v. 6*

THERE'S SOMETHING SPECIAL about a bonfire on the beach—
or at a campground or in the backyard, for that matter.
Gathering driftwood or scraps of kindling. Arranging a pile of
mismatched rocks into a barrier suitable for a firepit. Lighting
a match and sending logs into a blaze of orange flames accented
by golden sparks. *Magic.*

I love watching as the sky becomes a sort of fire in itself—a
dramatic painting of swirled oranges and pinks—while the
gilded flames of my fire lick at the rapidly cooling evening air.
Snuggling deeper into a woolly blanket as the stars come out.
Roasting a marshmallow (or two or three) and making sticky,

delicious sandwiches complete with white chocolate and short-bread cookies.

But in his second letter to his apprentice Timothy, the apostle Paul was talking about a very different sort of fire. He wasn't referring to a casual, cozy bonfire on the beach but to an all-encompassing flame. The kind that is meant to burn within the hearts of all who follow the Lord Jesus Christ.

Paul exhorted Timothy to fan his unique, God-given gift of ministry from a spark into a flame. To grow the heavenly talent he possessed into something greater—something with purpose. Something that would lead to a life spent boldly chasing after all that the Lord had for him.

In this letter, Paul also encouraged his young friend with these words: "The Spirit God gave us does not make us timid, but gives us power, love and self-discipline" (1:7). The special gifts that *we* have been given through Christ were not bestowed upon us so we could hide them away but so we could use them and grow them into something amazing.

Friends, God has given us *so many* gifts, most significantly the gifts of eternal life and salvation—which we can share with the whole world! He's also given us gifts that we can use to show God's love in even the most mundane moments of every day.

These gifts are beautiful and unique—service, hospitality, wisdom, encouragement, and more—but if we're not careful, they could end up fizzling out or burning down to coals in our hearts. Instead, we should do as Paul encouraged Timothy and fan the spark of our faith into a flame. One that burns deep in our hearts so strong and for so long that eventually it begins to spread, person to person, until our entire friend group experiences the warmth that comes from knowing Jesus Christ.

Because if a crackling bonfire on a breezy beach is magic, imagine the joy found in the spiritual gifts that come from God.

Dear Lord, thank you for all of the incredible and unique gifts you've given me. Help me to use these gifts to glorify you and bring joy to others. Help me not to let them die out, but instead fan them into a flame so my light will burn brightly for all the world to see. Amen.

How bright is your light? List your God-given gifts on one side, then the different ways you have been using them on the other. How could you do more for others with the talents and abilities God has given you?

_____

_____

_____

_____

_____

_____

DAY 4: A ROAD THROUGH THE FOG

READ PROVERBS 16:1-9

> *Commit to the LORD whatever you do,*
> *and he will establish your plans. ~ v. 3*

WHEN MY MOM AND I took a cruise down the Pacific coastline, we had to wake up long before dawn and drive more than an hour into the city just to catch the train that would take us to our ship's dock in Seattle. We had everything planned down to the second, and we left home in plenty of time that morning . . . or so we thought.

When we pulled onto the freeway, our car was immediately ensconced in fog. And I'm not talking about the kind of fog that clears within a couple of minutes. This was the cloaking, choking fog that makes you question the identity of objects that are only a few feet beyond your windshield. It was terrifying, making our way down the freeway, not knowing what lay beside or beyond us. But we also feared that we could miss our entire trip. So on we drove, by faith and not by sight, and with a lot of prayers thrown in.

Sometimes life feels a little like that foggy trip down the interstate—we might know where we're going but not exactly how to get there. The immediate future might look unclear even if we know where we're eventually supposed to end up. That's where God's plan comes in.

When we're wholeheartedly committed to following the

path God has laid out for us and honoring him above all else, he will help us on our journey and guide us through even the thickest fog of confusion or indecision. In today's passage, we read that when we fully commit our way to the Lord he will establish our path and guide our steps through life.

It can be scary to release control like that. It's much easier to white-knuckle the steering wheel as we drive through rain and fog than to lift up our hands and give everything over to the Lord, but our God is *such* an incredible Guide. His vision penetrates even the thickest cloud and darkest night. He is all-knowing, all-seeing, and all-loving. His plans for us are for good and not evil.

We've learned all this and more together over the past weeks, but it can be hard to put it into action—to really believe that God is guiding us through the journey of our life. When we do find the strength and courage to fully rely on our Savior, it frees us to run, unencumbered, down the path the Lord has laid out.

On that foggy morning years ago, my mom and I made it to the train station with time to spare despite the fact that we might as well have been driving through a bowl of pea soup. Similarly, we can always reach our final destination as long as we have God's help. When we fully trust in him and release our grip on the wheel of our life, we'll be amazed by what he does.

Today, let's take a deep breath, say a prayer, and let him take the wheel. Because if we do that, we'll be embarking on the greatest journey of our life.

Dear God, it's hard to see what the future will bring, and that can be downright terrifying. Please give me the courage to surrender my way to you, and guide me today. I know your way is better than mine, even if I can't see it right now. Amen.

....

What parts of your life feel foggy today? How can surrendering these areas of uncertainty to the Lord make your path clearer?

_____

_____

_____

_____

_____

_____

DAY 5: CASTLE WALLS

READ PSALM 71

> *As for me, I will always have hope;*
> *I will praise you more and more. ~ v. 14*

I HAVE ALWAYS wanted to visit a palace. Whether a fairy-tale castle in Germany, a Japanese *shiro*, or an ancient Mayan citadel, the idea of walking down narrow halls, peering out of towers to the ground far below, and climbing twisty-turny staircases makes my nerves zing with excitement. Not only are these ancient fortresses around the world beautifully made, they're sturdy, too. They've stood the test of time and now beckon visitors to stay awhile and soak in their history and lore.

While it's not all that easy to travel to a famous castle, we have the opportunity to visit a different kind of fortress whenever we need or want to. The psalmist in today's passage describes the Lord as his "rock of refuge . . . my fortress" (verse 3). This might not seem quite as exciting as exploring a palace, but our ability to find comfort from the Lord at any time of day is even more awe-inspiring.

Castles from days gone by were nearly impenetrable—and so is the love of God. Our Father really *is* a strong fortress. He has wrapped his huge, loving arms around us and given us the protection that we need as we journey down the road of life. And, because of this, our hearts can forever be filled with an unending hope in God our Father. That is why, as the psalmist says, he is so worthy of our praise.

God has given us each a path to walk in this life, but he hasn't asked us to go the distance alone. He hasn't sent us out into the woods with nothing more than a pat on the back. He is always with us—a refuge we can run to whenever we need help. Even in the middle of the darkest night or most fearsome challenge, the Lord is there.

And so, though I'd still love to visit a castle someday, I can find great peace and joy in a different kind of fortress. The one made from the embrace of a Father. The one I can go to for any reason, at any time. The one that will never crumble or decay.

Dear God, thank you for the ability to rest in you. I'm so grateful that you are my fortress. Please keep me safe in your arms forever. Amen.

....

What worries and cares would you like to leave in the walls of God's unending love today?

_____

_____

_____

_____

_____

_____

_____

_____

_____

_____

_____

_____

_____

DAY 6: CALLED TO THE JOURNEY

READ GENESIS 12:1-9

> *I will make you into a great nation, and I will bless you;*
> *I will make your name great, and you will be a blessing.* ~ v. 2

FOR ALL MY TALK of travel and adventuring, I'm actually quite fond of my very own home. In my twenty years here on this earth, I've lived in the same house in the same town in the same state . . . and I love it. I've never been tempted to go away to summer camp or even college—I did that online! In other words, if God came down and spoke to me and told me to leave everything I knew and loved . . . I probably wouldn't handle it very well.

The meekness and devotion of Abram (or Abraham, as we come to know him later in the Bible) is truly amazing. In today's passage, we get to witness his incredible faithfulness and bravery in action when Abram (who's *grandpa-aged*, by the way) is called to leave his home to go on a long journey. And he does it!

This kind of courage and faith is so inspirational to me. I love to think that I would do the same thing if God asked it of me, but, truth is, I would be terrified. Thank goodness that God has a unique plan for each of us, am I right?

Even though God hasn't asked all of us to go on a journey quite as daunting as Abraham's, we are all called to do hard things. While that looks different for everyone, we can know this: our lives as Christ followers won't always be easy, but they *will* be beautiful.

Abram, who was asked to leave all that he knew and start afresh at the ripe old age of seventy-five, clung to the promises that God left with him—promises of great blessings and miracles and a legacy that stretched far beyond his wildest imaginings.

We, too, have promises to cling to. I've shared some of my favorites with you over the last nine chapters, but there are so many more—an entire book of them, in fact. Abram stepped out in faith, with only a few of the Lord's words to guide his way. We have more than seven hundred *thousand* of them in the Bible. Abram was born long before Jesus walked the earth. We can know Jesus as our Lord and Savior. Abram was old, nearing the end of his life. We have years stretched before us like a newly unrolled map.

We are living lives of great potential and possibility—and God is right there, walking alongside us. No matter how daunting the road ahead of us appears, we can trust that it is all part of God's perfect plan.

The Lord had something amazing in store for Abram, and he has something great planned for us, too.

The journey might be long, friends, but it is *so* worth it.

Dear God, thank you for your promises that stand the test of time. Even when I'm called to do hard things, I love that I can rest in your words. Thank you for loving me so well and for giving me the strength to walk down the path you've paved for me. Amen.

Which of God's words are speaking to you the most during this leg of your journey? Use the space below to write or draw one of your favorite Bible verses.

DAY 7: WHAT HE HAS IN STORE

READ JOHN 15:18-25

I have chosen you out of the world. - v. 19

IF IT WERE up to me, I'd quit my day job right now and book a ticket around the world with one of my closest friends. God's creation is so *incredible*. I want to see all of it—meet all the people, eat all the food, and explore every corner of the planet. God's creativity is on display everywhere, and some days, it just feels criminal to sit in my living room when I know there's so much majesty to explore! (Other times you couldn't pry me away from my couch with a crowbar.)

That's why I love taking day trips even within my own city. An afternoon spent hiking and marveling at the power of a crashing waterfall or strolling down a tree-lined street helps center me and remind me of the one who gifted us all with the lives we call our own.

Our world is so wide and wonderful and amazing—the shortest afternoon walk can be filled with wonder when we know where to look. Yet the most impressive vistas and vibrant sunrises pale in comparison to what God has in store for us. The Lord saves us for a special purpose—not only to serve him in this life but also to glorify him forever. The earth as it is today is only a dim shadow of the glories awaiting us in eternity. The beauty we see, the joy we experience, will pale in comparison to the glory and majesty of all that is to come.

The Lord wants us, and he's laid his heavenly claim on our hearts. He has big things planned for us—things that will bring him glory and help the rest of the world experience his incredible love.

Of course, that's not always easy. Jesus made it clear in today's passage that many people who despise the Lord won't look too kindly upon us. The world doesn't welcome us with open arms because we're different. And that's okay.

We might face trials and persecution in this life because of our beliefs. Others might not understand why we'd choose to spend time with classmates who don't have many friends, abstain from certain activities, or spend Sunday mornings in church. But we can walk boldly with the Lord, knowing that he desires for us to follow him.

God set us apart as members of his Kingdom, as instrumental players in his glorious plan. No matter the struggles we face here in this world, the Lord is watching out for us. He chose us for this special purpose, and all of our days are already recorded in his book.

We are holy. We are chosen. We are beloved.

Dear God, sometimes I feel out of place in this world. Help me to remember what and who I'm living for—not for anything in this life but for everything in the life to come. Give me the strength to do all that you have called me to do today. Amen.

How can you show others a small piece of the glories that wait for them when Jesus returns and makes all things new? How can you help lead those people closer to Jesus today?

_____

_____

_____

_____

_____

_____

_____

_____

DAY 8: LEAP OF FAITH

READ HABAKKUK 2:1-4

> *The righteous person will live by his faithfulness. – v. 4*

AS A FREE-SPIRITED TRAVELER, I have to live by faith in many different ways. I must have faith that the pilot knows where he's going and won't crash into a random field. I have to believe that my luggage will end up in the right place at the right time. And I have to trust the restaurant reviews of those who have gone before me when I choose where to eat.

I remember a certain restaurant in Maui that my mom and I had walked by countless times on several different visits to the island. I'd read about it in my favorite dog-eared travel guide more times than I could count, and I'd always heard glowing reviews about the eatery. But it didn't have a view of the water, for one thing, and—for another—it was *French*! Who in their right mind would waste a balmy Hawaiian evening at a fussy French restaurant?

Well, thanks to a monsoon-style rainstorm that made eating at any of the open-air restaurants legitimately impossible, I ended up taking a step of faith and trusting what I'd read in innumerable reviews—that this bit of France in Lahaina would be a good choice for dinner.

My leap of faith paid off.

All these years later, I can still almost taste the seared fresh-caught fish and rich, decadent butter sauce. And the dessert! Layers of whipped cream, lemon curd, and enough puff pastry to make this sugar lover's heart swoon. It's a good thing you can't see me right now because I am positively *drooling*.

But that's another story.

What I'm saying is this: sometimes we have to take a mighty leap of faith in order to experience the greatest rewards of our lives. Sometimes stepping out in faith—even when we're not sure what in the world we're doing—results in incredible blessings.

This is especially true when it comes to our walk with God. Today's key verse from Habakkuk drives that home. "The righteous person will live by his faithfulness." If we truly love and trust in the Lord, we have no excuse for living in fear or walking in the ways of the world. Instead, we can stand strong and tall and walk joyfully in the way that God has laid out for us.

Jesus Christ not only rescued us from our sins—He gave our lives power and purpose. The power to make a difference, and the purpose that puts breath in our lungs. When we walk in faith, we're fulfilling all the plans the Lord has for us.

We are doing the will of God.

Dear Lord, help me to always live by faith in you. Whatever plans you have for me, I know they're absolutely amazing. Help me to always honor you by submitting to your will and trusting in your plans. Amen.

....

Do you live by faith, or do you only trust what you can see? Think about how you can exhibit the sort of "blind faith" exemplified by so many of the people in the Bible.

_____

_____

_____

_____

_____

_____

_____

DAY 9: GOOD WORK

READ PHILIPPIANS 1:3-11

> *He who began a good work in you will carry it on to completion until the day of Christ Jesus. ~ v. 6*

SOME DESTINATIONS take a long time to reach—I should know. I'll never forget quite how interminably long the flight between Los Angeles and London felt . . . fourteen hours had never seemed so endless! (What's worse, my mom managed to sleep half the trip away in the seat next to me. There was no jealousy there . . .)

Other journeys have taken even longer. I've spent days at sea aboard a cruise ship, traveling down various coastlines from one port to the next. I've passed other days shoved in the backseat of a car or peering out the window of a surprisingly slow-moving "bullet train."

But no trek through even the wildest wilderness could compare with the journey of a lifetime that we're traveling every second of every day.

The moment we trust in Jesus Christ and turn from our sins, we set off on a wild adventure that won't be truly over until we see Jesus face-to-face. As we travel through this life, the Lord will continually work in our hearts, molding our desires to reflect his own and moving through us to do all sorts of incredible things.

Before we start our journey with Jesus, we aren't able

to please God or do works that delight him. As soon as the Lord enters our lives, though, he invites us onto the path of purification. A path that we'll be on for the rest of our days. Sanctification—the process of becoming more and more like Jesus—is a slow, gradual undertaking that will never be truly complete in this life. But God will one day complete the mighty work he is doing in our hearts.

When we persevere through all things and honor the Lord in everything we do, we will see Christ carry out his good work in us. He will equip us to follow his will and boldly traverse the path he paved for us. Doing the will of our Father is a truly thrilling thing!

What good works are part of your life right now? Is the Lord using you to minister to a friend or family member, or is he ministering to *you* by helping you grow in grace and love for others? No matter what the Lord is doing in your life, cling tightly to him and bring him glory through the process.

The process of our refinement might take a while. It will certainly be the longest journey that any of us ever embark on. But the destination is nothing short of beautiful.

Dear Lord, what a journey my relationship with you has been so far! Thank you for walking through life with me and never failing to work in my heart and helping me grow closer to you. Please continue to sanctify and purify me. In your name I pray, amen.

....

Have you felt the Lord at work in or through you recently? What has that been like?

_____

_____

_____

_____

_____

_____

_____

_____

_____

DAY 10: STEADFAST

READ 1 CORINTHIANS 15:50-58

> _Therefore, my beloved brothers, be steadfast, immovable,_
> _always abounding in the work of the Lord, knowing that_
> _in the Lord your labor is not in vain. ~ v. 58 (esv)_

I LOVE that word—_steadfast._

When I think of it, my mind always goes back to pictures I've seen of incredible structures like the pyramids or ancient Mayan temples. I also remember the churches, cathedrals, and other historic buildings I visited in Europe. Some of these structures are nearly a thousand years old, yet they still stand firm in the hearts of great European cities. Thousands upon thousands of tourists visit these massive buildings each year, and congregations still worship within their walls.

These buildings are the very picture of *steadfast*. Immovable. Unwavering. Firm.

When we are steadfast, we're solid—not bowing to our own fears and desires or letting whispered words of temptation or doubt shake our foundation in Christ. When we stand firm in our faith, we're showing the world where our hope and trust are found—in the Lord Jesus. When we place our dreams and fears completely in the Father's hands, we are doing exactly what we're called to do—giving our lives completely to the One who gave us life in the first place.

A time is coming when everyone who knows and loves Jesus will walk into glory—a time when we will experience more joy than we could ever imagine. But until then, we have a job to do. We've been given *this* life on *this* earth for a special purpose.

God has a plan for each one of us, and it's truly amazing. It might not all make sense to us right now, but he is working behind the scenes to use our lives for his glory. That's why it's up to us to be steadfast. To stand firm in the faith and walk courageously down the path that God has laid out for us.

During this journey, there will be bumps in the road, forks in the path, and long layovers where we don't understand what the Lord is doing. Sometimes we'll barely be able to see the way in front of us through a cloud of mist, and other times God's plan will stretch out before us like a wide-open highway. No matter what, though, we can stand firm in our faith.

The gifts that the Lord has given us and the plans he has

for us are intended to show others what his Kingdom is like. We can stand firm and walk resolutely down the path God has revealed to us because we know our labor in the Lord is not in vain.

Dear God, thank you for the incredible road map you have given me. Thank you for crafting me uniquely and specially to do amazing things for your Kingdom. Please continue to lead and guide me in all that I do. Amen.

....

Is it ever hard for you to stand firm in the middle of the path God has laid out for you? What encourages you and helps you persevere?

_____

_____

_____

_____

_____

_____

_____

_____

bonus adventure: adventure awaits!

Congratulations . . . you've done it! You have completed your journey through nine chapters of God's incredible promises for your life. It is my hope and prayer that these devotions, journaling questions, and bonus adventures have helped you grow closer to the Lord *and* gain more of an understanding of what it looks like to follow him every step of your life. As I prepare to bid you farewell and send you out on the ultimate adventure—your walk with the Lord—I want to encourage you.

Over the last several weeks, you have been stretched and challenged to grow in your relationship with the Lord and truly chase after his will for your life. Hopefully you have been able to do that. Now, as you embark on the greatest journey, I have one final challenge for you.

I want you (yes, you!) to tell the world about the things you discovered in this devotional—about God's love and care for others and the unique, incredible road map he has given each and every one of us in his Word. I want you to use your own strengths and passions to help share his love with those around you. I want you to come alongside others not only as a traveling companion but as a junior tour guide, helping your friends and family members as they, too, live out the adventure to which God has called them.

How can you do this?

Let us count the ways . . .

If you, like me, love to write, consider starting a blog or social media account devoted to encouraging others in their walk with God. If you're musically talented, you could join the worship team at your church or get together a group of friends to form a small worship band. If you love to bake, think of how you could bless those around you with homemade goodies. Use your own God-given talents to share his love with others!

The following questions can help you as you ponder how to use your own gifts in this way. As you work through these questions, brainstorm how you can chase your dreams *and* make a real difference in your corner of the world.

- When do I feel closest to the Lord?

- How can I share my gifts with others in a way that reflects God's goodness?

- Have I felt the Lord leading me anywhere as I've walked through this devotional with him?

- Who in my community could benefit from an extra dose of encouragement?

- How can I go out of my way to encourage others on a daily basis?

- How am I living for Jesus Christ? Is my Spirit-filled life visible to other people? If not, how could I live more vibrantly for the Lord?

acknowledgments

WRITING THIS BOOK has been a journey of a lifetime—literally. When I began writing in my early teens, I had no idea that I had a devotional in me . . . and I didn't. Jesus, this book is for you—you gave me the words to speak and the wisdom to share. Without you, I am nothing. Thank you, Lord, for gifting me with this opportunity to share your heart with the world.

And thank *you*—yes, you. You reading this right now. If you picked up this devotional, took the time to go on an adventure with me, and read to the end, you have my unending gratitude. I'm so thankful that you picked *me* to spend time with as you sought the Lord and grew closer to him. Keep living for Jesus, and remember—even when we can't see the path we're on, God will show us which step to take.

But there wouldn't even have been a book to read if not for Linda Howard, who encouraged my devotional-writing efforts from day one and from whom I got "the call" I'd been waiting for; Danika King, who offered her amazing editing expertise and truly understood the heart behind this devotional; Alyssa

Clements, who showed so much encouragement and support; and everyone else on the wonderful Tyndale team. Thank you—all of you. I'm so incredibly grateful that you were willing to take a chance on me and pour your heart and soul into this project right alongside me.

To one of my greatest fans—my fiancé, Elias LaLande—thank you for your unending support and your enthusiasm for me as I've embarked on this exciting writing adventure.

Of course, no acknowledgments section will ever be complete without an extra-big shout-out to my mom. Not only is she my best friend and travel partner in crime, but she's also my biggest cheerleader (and my favorite proofreader). Mom, thanks for going with me on all of these crazy adventures and for walking with me through the wildest adventure of all—life. Kudos also to Dad, for being our airport chauffeur whenever we head off on our "girls' trips" and for giving me my love of the sea. I would never be writing these words right now if not for my incredible parents, so Mom and Dad, I hope you know it . . . you're the best!

about the author

TAYLOR BENNETT is a Jesus-loving, world-traveling lover of books, words, and stories. She received her first publishing contract at the age of seventeen, and she now seeks to inspire other young girls to reach for their own God-given dreams and do the impossible through him. Since that first contract, Taylor has gone on to publish several more books as well as articles with magazines such as *Devozine* and *Brio*. She loves connecting with young women both in person though speaking engagements and online via Instagram (@taylor.bennett.author).

You are a LIMITED EDITION!
A 30-Day Adventure toward Finding Joy in Who God Made You to Be
ALL-CAPS YOU
Sadie Robertson Huff
Emma Mae Jenkins
Foreword by Jennie Allen
Embrace the person God created YOU to be.
Available at Tyndale.com and your favorite booksellers.
CP1621

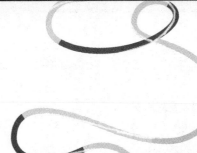

A MIXTAPE OF
BIG '80S STYLE,
HIGH SCHOOL ANGST,
AND A CLASSIC
JANE AUSTEN TALE

A. K. PITTMAN

a novel

PUDGE & PREJUDICE

wander™

CP1645

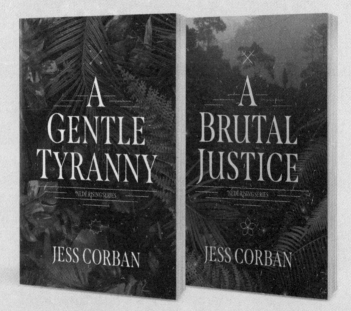

THE NEDÉ RISING SERIES

A Gentle Tyranny — Jess Corban

A Brutal Justice — Jess Corban

WHAT PATH WILL REINA CHOOSE?
AND WHAT WILL HER CHOICE COST HER?

wander
An imprint of
Tyndale House
Publishers

CP1635